Puerto Rico Relocation Guidebook

PRe

The Official PRelocate Guidebook, Second Edition

Copyright © 2022 by PRelocate, LLC

Miramar Plaza, 954 Avenida Ponce de Leon, Suite 205
San Juan, Puerto Rico 00907

https://relocatepuertorico.com

787-503-8184

The following content has been prepared for informational purposes only. It is not intended as, and does not constitute, legal advice nor tax advice nor the solicitation of any prospective client, and PRelocate, LLC, does not have any obligation to update any of the information contained herein.

About PRelocate

We started PRelocate to provide individuals and small businesses the knowledge and services they need to relocate to Puerto Rico. When moving to Puerto Rico ourselves, we were buried in a process that was difficult to understand and required dozens of hours of research, not to mention the added costs of professional services to clear things up. We believe that living and working in Puerto Rico is a tremendous opportunity that shouldn't be overlooked due to cost, disjointed information, or an overall lack of clarity.

Our goal is to enable and empower you to make a sound decision about whether Puerto Rico is right for you. If it is, we will make it happen for you in a straightforward, accurate, and economical way. We speak for the community in that we hope you join us here in beautiful Puerto Rico.

Quick Statistics on Our Team

Global Presence: The PRelocate team helps clients across the United States and worldwide relocate to Puerto Rico. Our team is on the ground, literally, which gives our team prescient, up-to-date information on Act 60 and other tax incentive programs. This allows us to provide strategic and informed advice to our clients on what is required to successfully relocate to Puerto Rico.

Business and Tax Strategy: Our team provides resources and consultations to help you learn if relocating to Puerto Rico is the right move for you. For the Act 60 export services tax application, our consultations are free which saves you thousands of dollars compared to working with a law firm. We work with you to advise and handle your Investor Resident Individual Tax application. In 90 percent of cases a standard framework is sufficient for getting through the application process. In the case that a lawyer or accountant is needed, we will bring one on.

Full Service Moving Support: We have grown our offering to include everything needed to move and settle into Puerto Rico, including: Real Estate support (both within PR and helping you sell in the US), moving support, a landing package to help get utilities set up, as well as many additional services. After going through the process ourselves without help we realized there was a better way to move to Puerto Rico.

Act 60 Approvals: As Act 60 recipients ourselves, we here at PRelocate have extensive experience on how to succeed through the Act 60 application process.

Samuel B. Silverman

Sam has extensive real estate development, management, financing, and brokerage experience in Florida, Pennsylvania, California, Georgia, Puerto Rico, and internationally in the People's Republic of China. In addition to founding PRelocate, Sam also co-founded EB5 Affiliate Network, one of the leading EB-5 Capital consulting companies and an EB-5 Fund Manager. Collectively, EB5AN manages over 1,800 EB-5 investors across 15 Regional Centers, representing nearly $1B of EB-5 Capital and over $3Bn of total real estate development. Prior to PRelocate and EB5AN, Sam served as the Director of Corporate Strategy and Expansion for Professional Golfer Jack Nicklaus in the People's Republic of China, living full time in Beijing. Sam was also previously employed by the Boston Consulting Group, one of the top management consulting and business strategy firms in the world, where he worked directly with Fortune 500 companies in the food service, media, manufacturing, hospitality, and real estate spaces in the United States, Europe, and Middle East. Sam was honored by *Entrepreneur360 Magazine* and was recognized by *Forbes Magazine* as a National Winner for the Forbes 30 Under 30 List of Social Entrepreneurs. Sam holds a B.A. in Economics with a concentration in Mandarin Chinese from Yale University, a certificate in Financial Accounting from the London School of Economics and Political Science, and an M.B.A. from the Stanford Graduate School of Business.

Michael Schoenfeld

Mike has extensive private equity investment, business diligence, management consulting, and entrepreneurship experience. In addition to PRelocate, Mike also founded EB5 Affiliate Network, one of the leading EB-5 Capital consulting companies and an EB-5 Fund Manager. Collectively, EB5AN manages over 1,800 EB-5 investors across 15 Regional Centers, representing nearly $1B of EB-5 Capital and over $3Bn of total real estate development. Mike previously worked for AEA Investors, a leading middle-market private equity firm with $10B under management, focused on making control-oriented investments in consumer goods, industrial goods, and business services companies. He invested out of their previous $2.5B middle market private equity fund. His completed transactions include the $2B LBO of 24 Hour Fitness, the leading fitness club operator with over 400 clubs nationwide, and the minority investment in Brand Networks, a leading social media marketing solutions provider. Mike was also previously employed by the Boston Consulting Group, one of the top management consulting and business strategy firms in the world, where he worked directly with Fortune 500 companies in the transportation, financial services, industrial goods, information, technology, and real estate spaces. Mike was also recognized by *Entrepreneur360 Magazine* and named a National Winner on *Forbes Magazine*'s 30 Under 30 List of Social Entrepreneurs. Mike holds a B.A. in Economics and a B.S. in Business Administration from the University of North Carolina at Chapel Hill.

Table of Contents

Topics for Act 60 Companies

Puerto Rico Tax Incentives Overview

The most famous tax incentives for incoming Americans are Act 20 and Act 22—now the "Export Services" and the "Investor Resident Individual" tax incentives, respectively, under the newly enacted Act 60—but Puerto Rico offers a variety of tax incentives that may fit your needs. Read our extensive list of Puerto Rican tax incentives to determine which is right for you. Please note that all incentives other than Act 22 (Individual Investor) are available to local Puerto Ricans as well as those moving to the Island. It is estimated over 30% of the Act 20 / Act 60 export service businesses are owned by local Puerto Ricans' that did not relocate under the tax incentives.

Export Services (Formerly Act 20)

The Export Services tax incentive is available to businesses established in Puerto Rico that offer services to customers or clients outside of Puerto Rico. Examples include research and development, consulting services, call centers, software development, and accounting services, among many others. A business must not provide services to the Puerto Rican market to be eligible for this tax incentive. Additionally, businesses that make or expect to make $3,000,000 per year must hire the equivalent of one full-time employee who is a Puerto Rican resident to be eligible. Manufacturing businesses must hire the equivalent of three full-time employees.

Tax advantages include:

- 4% fixed income tax rate (2% for the first five years of the decree if the business is in Vieques and Culebra)
- 100% tax exemption on dividends
- 50% tax exemption on municipal taxes (100% for the first five years of the decree if the business is in Vieques and Culebra)
- 100% tax exemption on municipal taxes in the first semester of business
- 75% tax exemption on property taxes (100% for the first five years of the decree if the business is in Vieques and Culebra)
- 100% tax exemption on property under construction
- 100% tax exemption on gross capital gains
- 75% tax exemption on construction excise tax
- 100% tax exemption on excise tax and sales and use tax

Export Trade and Hubs (Formerly Act 20)

The former Act 20, which focused on businesses established in Puerto Rico that exported their goods or services abroad, was split up into two separate acts in the newly enacted Act 60. With the Export Trade and Hubs act, Puerto Rico incentivizes eligible businesses that derive at least 80% of their gross income from the traffic or export of products. Eligible activities include reselling products to customers outside of Puerto Rico; selling or distributing intangible products, such as copyrights, patents, or digital content, to customers outside of Puerto Rico; storing, transporting, and distributing products of third parties; and assembling, bottling, and packaging goods for export outside of Puerto Rico.

Tax advantages include:

- 4% fixed income tax rate (2% for the first five years of the decree if the business is in Vieques and Culebra)
- 100% tax exemption on dividends
- 50% tax exemption on municipal taxes (100% for the first five years of the decree if the business is in Vieques and Culebra)
- 100% tax exemption on municipal taxes in the first semester of business
- 75% tax exemption on property taxes (100% for the first five years of the decree if the business is in Vieques and Culebra)
- 100% tax exemption on property under construction
- 100% tax exemption on gross capital gains
- 75% tax exemption on construction excise tax
- 100% tax exemption on excise tax and sales and use tax

Investor Resident Individual (Formerly Act 22)

One of the most well-known Puerto Rican tax incentives, the Investor Resident Individual tax incentive is available to any person who was not a resident of Puerto Rico for the 10 tax years preceding July 1, 2019, and who becomes a resident before December 1, 2035. To be eligible, investors must annually donate $10,000 to nonprofit entities in Puerto Rico. In Act 60, this decree was updated to include tax exemptions on capital gains from cryptocurrencies. Please note these rates apply to any gains earned AFTER establishing residency in Puerto Rico but do not eliminate previously earned but unrealized capital gains.

Tax advantages include:

- 0% taxation on capital gains
- 0% taxation on interest and dividends

Act 60 Summary

Export Services Tax Incentive – For Businesses

Business owners who establish a qualifying business in Puerto Rico can enjoy significant tax benefits:

- 4% corporate tax rate
- 100% tax exemption on distributions from earnings and profits
- 50% tax exemption on municipal taxes
- 75% tax exemption on municipal and state property taxes (small and medium businesses can receive a 100% exemption during their first five years of operation)

Owners of existing businesses can qualify for the Act 60 business tax incentives in one of two ways:
- Moving the entire company, including employees, to Puerto Rico and ceasing all operations in the United States
- Establishing a Puerto Rico subsidiary and recording the percentage of business income and expenses related to the Puerto Rico entity so that it can be taxed under the Act 60 incentives

Applying for the Export Services Act

You'll have to pay a one-time fee of $1,000 when you file your initial application. Then, you'll be required to file an annual report each year along with a $500 fee.

PRelocate is a qualified Promoter and assists with the application for Act 60 – Export Services Act. We aim to simplify the process and help clients understand the benefits of the program. For simple businesses our team can prepare everything needed. If there is additional complexity, we have a strong supporting team of attorneys and accountants that have been vetted by our team and have strong feedback from prior clients.

Investor Resident Individual Tax Incentive

The tax incentives enjoyed by Individual Resident Investors in Puerto Rico are perhaps the most impressive of all Puerto Rican tax incentives:

- 100% tax exemption from Puerto Rico income taxes on all dividends
- 100% tax exemption from Puerto Rico income taxes on all interest
- 100% tax exemption from Puerto Rico income taxes on all short-term and long-term capital gains

- 100% tax exemption from Puerto Rico income taxes on all cryptocurrencies and other crypto assets

Just keep in mind that to qualify for these generous incentives, you must become a bona fide resident of Puerto Rico.

Passing the Residency Tests

As a basic overview, here's what you must do to pass the three tests to establish bona fide residency in Puerto Rico:

- Be physically present in Puerto Rico for at least 183 days of each tax year
- Make Puerto Rico your tax home by establishing your office or primary place of work there
- Move your family and possessions to Puerto Rico, get a Puerto Rican driver's license, register to vote in Puerto Rico, and do other things that demonstrate your commitment to a life on the island

The Newest "Test" Outlined in Act 60

Puerto Rico now requires the purchase of real estate property within two years of obtaining your tax exemption decree. Two years should be plenty of time to decide where to live in Puerto Rico. The property must also remain the individual's primary residence throughout the validity of the decree.

Capital Gains Before Moving to Puerto Rico

Capital gains accrued prior to your move to Puerto Rico are treated differently depending on when they are recognized:

- Within 10 years, gains that appreciated prior to relocation will be taxable at the U.S. rate
- If the gains are recognized after 10 years of your move, they are taxed at Puerto Rico's preferential 5% flat tax rate, and you do not owe U.S. taxes on them

Applying for the Investor Resident Individual Act

There is a $5,000 fee due with your application, which you are to submit to the Office of Industrial Tax Exemption. Upon approval, you will be required to pay a one-time $5,000 acceptance fee. Afterward, each year, you will have to make a $10,000 charitable donation and submit an annual report along with a $5,000 fee.

Changes Between Act 20/22 and Act 60

Former governor of Puerto Rico Ricardo Rosselló signed Act 60–2019, commonly known as the Puerto Rico Incentives Code, into law on July 1, 2019, with an effective date of January 1, 2020. The Incentives Code consolidates various tax decrees, incentives, subsidies, and benefits, including Act 20, the Act to Promote the Export of Services, and Act 22, the Act to Promote the Relocation of Individual Investors to Puerto Rico. We have reviewed the language of the new law and are pleased to share the major changes to the Act 20 and 22 programs below.

Export Services (Previously known as Act 20)

- **Employee requirement**: Under the new law, exempt businesses that generate an annual business volume of at least $3,000,000 must also directly employ at least one full-time employee. The employee must be a Puerto Rican resident and directly participate in the business activities pertinent to the decree.
- **Audit by OITE**: Under the new law, the Office of Industrial Tax Exemption (OITE) will perform an independent audit of exempt businesses at least every two years. *Please note: It is unclear if this will apply to Act 20's established prior to the new incentive code.*
- **Blockchain**: Under the new law, Blockchain-related services are specifically included as an eligible business activity.
- **Reduction of property taxes**: Under the new law, exempt businesses will enjoy a seventy-five percent (75%) exemption on the municipal and state property taxes during the validity of the decree. Businesses that qualify as "Small and Medium Businesses" (PYMES, by its Spanish acronym) will also enjoy 100% exemption on municipal and state property taxes during their first five years of operation.
- **Reduction of municipal taxes**: Under the new law, the exempt businesses will enjoy a fifty percent (50%) exception on municipal contributions or municipal patents applicable to eligible services provided by the businesses during the validity of the decree.

Investor Resident Individual (Previously known as Act 22)

- **Annual charitable donation**: Under the new law, grantees will need to make a $10,000 annual charitable donation – $5,000 of that donation will go to a government-approved list of charities and $5,000 may go to any Puerto Rican charity of your choice.
- **Real estate requirement**: Under the new law, grantees must purchase – within two years of obtaining the decree – real estate property in Puerto Rico, which shall be the grantee's primary residence throughout the validity of the decree. Based on our interpretation, this purchased real estate property cannot be rented out.

- **Crypto and other crypto assets**: Under the new law, cryptocurrencies and other crypto assets are explicitly included as eligible for tax exemption.

General Changes

- **Validity of the decrees**: Under the new law, the initial decree is granted for a term of 15 years and may be extended for an additional 15 years.
- **DDEC Annual Report**: Under the new law, The Department of Economic Development and Commerce of Puerto Rico (DDEC, by its Spanish acronym) will publish a yearly report on all the tax incentives requested and granted. The report will include the name of the business and principal shareholders, the date the decree was granted, name of the municipality where the business operates, number of jobs created by the business, etc. *Please note: It is unclear if this will apply to decrees established prior to the new incentive code.*

From January 2020, the initial decree will be granted for a term of 15 years, compared to the current 20 years, and may be extended for an additional 15 years, compared to the current 10. Furthermore, the Department of Economic Development and Commerce of Puerto Rico, also known by the Spanish acronym DDEC, will publish a yearly report on all the incentives requested and granted. The report will include the name of the business and principal shareholders, the date the decree was granted, the name of the municipality in which the business operates, and the number of jobs created by the business.

While the consolidation of the decrees, incentives, subsidies, and benefits governing taxation in Puerto Rico improves transparency, it introduces more rigid, restrictive, and expensive requirements. According to Pilar Rivera, Operations Manager at PRelocate, "The changes to Acts 20 and 22 applied only to applications submitted after December 31, 2019." She further urged those who are interested in the program to consult an attorney for advice on specific legal and tax issues.

14

Best Strategies to Benefit From Act 60

Sell Assets Strategically to Best Take Advantage of Act 60 Tax Benefits

On top of the extra money you get to keep, the Act 60 Investor Resident Individual decree offers a unique opportunity to investors: the ability to continually sell and rebuy assets without any negative tax impacts. This allows you to reset your tax basis higher and higher, which can prove useful when the asset's price is increasing. Though the tax basis doesn't matter as long as the tax benefits apply to you, since you pay a 0% tax rate, setting your basis higher can be important if you lose the tax exemption benefits. This could happen for a number of reasons—for instance, your tax decree could be revoked due to non-compliance, Puerto Rico could become a state, Congress could revise the tax law to have Puerto Rican residents pay mainland taxes, Congress could change the rules to determine Puerto Rico-sourced capital gains, or the Puerto Rican government could amend the program in a way that makes compliance prohibitively expensive.

Resetting your tax basis can also help if you're unsure whether a particular gain is sourced from Puerto Rico or the United States. If you hold a position for many years and sell it for a large gain, you may find that income subject to mainland taxes if the IRS decides you didn't qualify as a bona fide Puerto Rican resident for the year of the gain. However, if you sell and rebuy your asset each year, you limit the risk of having to pay U.S. taxes due to IRS determinations to annual gains rather than all the gains on the asset since your initial purchase.

As long as the asset's value increases materially, you should not experience any downside to selling and rebuying it. It should be possible to buy the asset again after just a few minutes or hours. It's recommended to set a reminder for yourself to sell and rebuy your assets at least once each year [we recommend in December], but it would also be a good idea to do it whenever a volatile asset shoots up in price. Cryptocurrency is a prime example.

Before employing this strategy, we strongly recommend establishing residency in Puerto Rico and consulting a tax advisor to determine whether gains on the asset in question can indeed be considered Puerto Rico-sourced and whether federal bifurcation rules apply to it. Additionally, if you're planning to fully commit to Puerto Rico long term—to the extent that your bona fide residency will be obvious and not disputed by the IRS—this may not be the best strategy, because if you hold an asset for 10 years and fulfill the bona fide residency requirements for the entire period, a reduced long-term capital gains rate of 5% would apply on any gains sourced in the United States prior to establishing Puerto Rico residency. This reduced 5% rate is substantially lower than the normal capital gains rate for long-term capital gains sourced exclusively in the

United States, which as of the publication date of this guidebook varies between 18.8%-23.8% with the full Medicare Contribution Tax (with additional City and State taxes depending on your location within the United States).

Act 60 Residency Requirements

Those considering taking advantage of Puerto Rico's generous tax exemptions without committing to a life on the island, be warned—integrating into Puerto Rican life isn't just a bonus. It's a requirement.

Puerto Rico offers a myriad of tax incentives, but they all entail the same goal for the government: boosting Puerto Rico's economy by attracting to the island high-net-worth individuals who will invest in the infrastructure. Thus, to reap the benefits of the ever-popular Act 60 Export Services and Investor Resident Individual tax exemptions, you must hold up your end of the bargain and settle into a life in Puerto Rico. Bona fide residency is the benchmark to determine commitment to the island, and it is measured by three tests: the presence test, the tax home test, and the closer connection test. All three are easy to satisfy if you truly commit to a new life in Puerto Rico.

The Presence Test

The presence test considers how much time you spend in Puerto Rico. The IRS is primarily concerned about how much time a decree holder spends in Puerto Rico compared to in the United States, so feel free to travel abroad—just be wary of how much time you spend in the United States.

The IRS offers five different conditions a decree holder can use to fulfill the presence requirement for bona fide residency. You don't need to satisfy them all—satisfying just a single one is sufficient. Two revolve around the number of days a decree holder is present in Puerto Rico throughout the tax year:
- Spending at least 183 days in Puerto Rico throughout the tax year

- Spending at least 549 days in Puerto Rico throughout the current and previous two tax years, including at least 60 days per tax year

The remaining three concentrate not on a decree holder's connections to Puerto Rico but rather their lack of connections to the United States:
- Spending no more than 90 days in the United States throughout the tax year
- Earning no more than $3,000 in the United States **and** spending more days in Puerto Rico than in the United States throughout the tax year
- Having no significant connections to the United States throughout the tax year

Making the presence test a little easier is the fact that a "presence day" in Puerto Rico counts any day in which you are physically present in Puerto Rico, even if just briefly. Even if you're only in Puerto Rico for an hour on a certain day, that counts as being present in Puerto Rico.

Another bonus is the 30 free international travel days decree holders are eligible for if they spend more time in Puerto Rico than the United States. These free travel days encompass travel outside of the United States but effectively mean that a decree holder need only spend 153 days in Puerto Rico, as long as the extra 30 days are spent **outside** of the United States. Note, however, that if you're going for the "549 days in a three-year period" condition, you must still physically spend at least 60 days in Puerto Rico each year.

Finally, exceptions are available for special circumstances, such as medical treatment or disasters.

The most common way the presence test is met is through the 183 days a year in Puerto Rico. Please remember that being in Puerto Rico for 183 days alone is NOT enough – you also need to meet the Tax Home Test and the Closer Connection Test.

The Tax Home Test

The tax home test is far more straightforward than the presence test and only encompasses a single condition: maintain your tax home in Puerto Rico throughout the entire tax year. Your tax home is the jurisdiction in which your primary place of employment is located. Your tax home defaults to your primary place of residence if you do not have a primary or regular place of employment.

Basically, to satisfy the tax home test, keep your office—or your home, as the case may be—in Puerto Rico.

The Closer Connection Test

The closer connection test can be tricky for some Act 60 decree holders to satisfy because it's subjective and offers no hard guidelines on fulfillment. The closer connection test simply seeks to determine whether an Act 60 decree holder maintains closer connections to Puerto Rico or the United States and uses a number of factors to determine one's national ties, such as the following:

- Where they live
- Where their spouse and children, if any, live
- Where they keep important personal belongings, such as their car or furniture
- What jurisdiction their primary bank is in
- Where they primarily conduct business
- What jurisdiction their driver's license is issued by
- Where they are registered to vote
- Where the organizations they affiliate with are located

Naturally, some of these factors are more important than others—the IRS will especially consider where a decree holder's spouse and children live. Selling or renting out your home in the United States is also a good idea, as not having a home readily available in the United States will certainly boost your standing in the assessment of a closer connection.

Ultimately, you can satisfy the closer connection test however works best for you and your circumstances, but fully committing to a new life in Puerto Rico is the simplest solution. Many of the factors that help you pass the closer connection test, such as a Puerto Rican driver's license or voter registration, will also help you get by in day-to-day life in Puerto Rico.

The Newest "Test" Outlined in Act 60

Puerto Rico now requires the purchase of real estate property within two years of obtaining your tax exemption decree. Two years should be plenty of time to decide where to live in Puerto Rico. The property must also remain the individual's primary residence throughout the validity of the decree.

The "Year of the Move" Exception

Given that one of the requirements for bona fide Puerto Rican residency is to maintain a tax home in Puerto Rico for the entire tax year, satisfying this test in the year of your move is clearly impossible unless you move on January 1. That's why the IRS has introduced a special exception for your first year in Puerto Rico, contingent on three conditions:

- Maintaining a tax home in Puerto Rico for the last 183 days of the year
- Not having been a bona fide resident of Puerto Rico in the three tax years before the year of the move
- Achieving bona fide residency in the year of the move and the two years following it

This means that as long as you move to Puerto Rico before July 1, you can become a bona fide Puerto Rican resident in your first year on the island and reap the benefits of your Act 60 decree immediately.

Don't Pass Up a Lucrative Life in Puerto Rico

Puerto Rico's bona fide residency tests may seem intimidating, but if you're dedicated to starting fresh in the United States' Caribbean island territory, the tests are simple. With beautiful, sunny weather, a vibrant Hispanic culture, and generally lower prices than in the mainland, Puerto Rico offers more than just tax savings. And since its generous tax incentives are only available to bona fide residents, enjoying the wonders of a Puerto Rican life is imperative. In more ways than one, starting a new life in Puerto Rico can be the best investment you ever make.

Eligibility Guidelines for Export Services Tax Advantages

In an effort to accelerate economic recovery in Puerto Rico, the Puerto Rican government has provided generous business tax incentives for eligible service industry entities, ranging from accountants and ad agencies to hedge funds and other consulting firms, for nearly nine years. The initial iteration of this legislation came in the form of Act 20 in January 2012.

In sum, Act 20 stipulated an extremely low (4%) corporate tax rate for Puerto Rico businesses operating *within* the territory's borders on all income received from clients based *outside* of its borders. So, the first eligibility requirement for businesses seeking the tax break was that a business would have to offer remote service capabilities. In other words, the Act asked whether a business owner and its employees could work from Puerto Rico and still provide services to customers outside Puerto Rican borders.

One of the primary advantages of this legislation to the Puerto Rican economy was that the United States has special treatment for US Territories that are not States. The responsibility of taxation in many ways is left up to the Puerto Rican government itself.

Key Eligibility Requirements for Puerto Rico-based Operations

First, understand that the term "operations inside of Puerto Rico" means that whatever a business's value or work output may be, the product must have been created on Puerto Rican soil. Once a business owner determines that they qualify based on the location of their business, there is another set of key eligibility requirements to consider:

- Every business owner and employee must be paid a reasonable salary for the work they do.
- The income that owners and employees are paid must be taxed at the ordinary income tax rate for Puerto Rico (sometimes reaching 33%). A business cannot pass through *all* of its net revenue at the corporate tax rate of 4%.
- Act 60 businesses are subject to independent audits once every two years at a minimum by the Office of Industrial Tax Exemption (OITE). Businesses established who filed for the Act 20 version of the incentive may also be subject to the audits, but that has not been clarified to date.
- Businesses generating $3M+ annually are required to directly employ at least one Puerto Rican resident who directly participates in business activities explicitly related to its offerings.

Act 60 Export Services Businesses May Not Have a Nexus with Puerto Rico

Business owners often question whether they may have clients both inside *and* outside of Puerto Rico and still qualify for this export services tax incentive. The short answer is not on the income derived from Puerto Rican clients. To be eligible for the tax break, the legislation says a business must not have a nexus with Puerto Rico. This means the services a business provides cannot be related in any way to the conduct of trade, business, or other activities *inside* Puerto Rico.

At its core, this requirement stipulates that any client of a Puerto Rico-based business must be located outside the territory. To clarify, here is a list of disqualified entities (as they are considered to "have a nexus" with Puerto Rico):

- Any business or entity that has participated in income-producing activities within Puerto Rico for other Puerto Rico customers
- When a sale of any property for use, consumption, or disposition in Puerto Rico has occurred and the income for those activities is derived from money already inside of the territory
- Businesses who have lobbied on the regulations, laws, and/or administrative duties of the Puerto Rican government or its instrumentalities
- Businesses that have directly counseled on the regulations, laws, and/or administrative duties of the Puerto Rican government or any of its instrumentalities
- Entities participating in any activities directly designated by the Puerto Rico Secretary of the Department of Economic Development

There are nearly two dozen categories of businesses that are eligible and can qualify as an Act 60 business. Business owners with specific questions regarding the eligibility of their company and other requirements for the Export Services tax incentive should reach out to us at PRelocate for help. We can advise you, for example, on how to secure a business's tax exemption decree, determine whether all or only part of your business's operations should be transferred, and ensure all other eligibility requirements are being met.

Domicile and Non-Domicile Compliance

If you have moved to Puerto Rico to take advantage of the Act 60 tax incentives, you will be required to provide various forms of evidence of your bona fide residence on the island. One form of evidence you can use is declarations of domicile and non-domicile.

What Is the Declaration of Domicile?

The declaration of domicile is a formal document recognizing Puerto Rico as your official, legal territory of bona fide long-term residence. The document specifies your full name, the date you became a bona fide resident, your Puerto Rican address, your former city of residence, and the date on which you have executed the document. The document must be signed, sealed, and delivered in the presence of witnesses, who must provide their signatures, and must be sworn before a public notary, commissioner of oaths, or solicitor.

What Is the Declaration of Non-Domicile?

The declaration of non-domicile is a formal document recognizing your cessation of long-term residence at your previous state of domicile. The document specifies your full name, your previous city of residence, your Puerto Rican address, the date you became a bona fide Puerto Rican resident, and the date on which you have executed the document. The document must be signed, sealed, and delivered in the presence of witnesses, who must provide their signatures, and must be sworn before a public notary, commissioner of oaths, or solicitor.

Why Is the Declaration of Domicile Important?

The declaration of domicile helps prove that you are a bona fide resident of Puerto Rico, which is a requirement of the Act 60 tax exemption program. After meeting the requirements of bona fide residency—spending at least 183 days of a given year on the island, making Puerto Rico your tax home, and having a closer connection to Puerto Rico than the United States or another country—you should execute a declaration of domicile to officially change your domicile.

Residency and domicile are not the same thing. Your residence is a home you intend to inhabit temporarily, whereas your domicile is your permanent home. For many people, these overlap, but it is important to declare Puerto Rico as not only your residence but also your domicile, indicating to the Puerto Rican government that you intend to reside long-term on the island.

Why Is the Declaration of Non-Domicile Important?

The declaration of non-domicile serves as an official document informing your former state of domicile that you no longer intend to reside there long term. State domicile regulations differ from state to state, but in some states, a declaration of non-domicile is important to void your income tax status in that state. Furthermore, in the United States, it is not possible to have multiple domiciles at the same time, so declaring your non-domicile in your previous state is necessary to declare domicile in Puerto Rico.

Act 60 Donation Requirements

In addition to establishing bona fide residency in Puerto Rico, one of the requirements of the Act 22 (now Act 60 investor Resident individual) program is a yearly donation to a Puerto Rican charity or nonprofit organization. Under Act 22, the required donation amount was $5,000, but this has jumped to $10,000 under the newly enacted Act 60. While investors are more or less free to choose the organization they donate to, there are some rules to which they have to pay attention.

Act 60 Investors

Act 60 investors are required to donate double the amount that Act 22 decree holders donate, but the donation is split into two parts—a donation of $5,000 to two different organizations is required under Act 60. Like with Act 22 donations, the nonprofit entities must operate in Puerto Rico and not be run by the investor or their family, spouse, or partner. Act 60 investors must also submit their donation before December 31 and present proof in their annual report in May.

The first $5,000 must go to a nonprofit organization listed by Comisión Especial Conjunta de Fondos Legislativos para Impacto Comunitario (CECFL), which publishes an annual list with approved organizations. This list is posted to the PRelocate website annually.

The second $5,000 can go to any Puerto Rican nonprofit entity of the investor's choice, as long as it falls under Section 1101.01 of the Puerto Rico Internal Revenue Code. This allows for a broader pool than Act 22's restriction of donations to Section 1101.01 (a) (2)–certified nonprofits. One point to bear in mind, however, is that the organization cannot be on CECFL's list.

Nonprofits Certified Under Section 1101.01 (a) (2)

To facilitate the donation process for Act 22 and 60 investors, we've created a list of nonprofits certified under Section 1101.01 (a) (2) that qualify as a recipient for your required yearly donation. All these organizations have certification from both the Puerto Rican government and the IRS, which we have collected and can present to clients upon request.

The 20/22 Act Society

The 20/22 Act Society was formed by one of the first individuals to take advantage of Puerto Rico's tax incentives as a way to unify those interested in relocating to the island and those who have already made the move. The Society works to show the positive impact these acts can have in Puerto Rico's nonprofit sector, supporting and working with local charities to help Puerto Rico's children, elderly, homeless, and animals, among others.

Website: https://www.the2022actsociety.org/
Email: info@the2022actsociety.org

The HERA Institute

The HERA Institute was founded by female entrepreneurs and business professionals whose mission is to promote female entrepreneurship through education, mentoring, and community. The nonprofit works with local women and their communities to provide educational, financial, and social support, along with career and business advancement courses and programs at no cost to our students. Donations go towards funding scholarships, seminars, small female-owned business funding, job fairs, and much more.

Website: www.herainstitute.org
Email: info@herainstitute.org

Caribbean Thoroughbred Aftercare, Inc.

Thoroughbred racehorses from the United States are regularly shipped to Puerto Rico and other Caribbean islands to partake in races. Caribbean Thoroughbred Aftercare's mission is to ensure these horses continue to enjoy a safe, healthy life after retirement, including by repatriating them to the United States.

Website: https://www.ctahorse.com
Email: caribbeanottb@gmail.com

ProTechos

ProTechos rebuilds damaged roofs in Puerto Rico for communities and individuals in need. The nonprofit works with grassroots organizations to identify and prioritize the most urgent cases, and as they work to restore roofs, they teach local volunteers construction skills to help address the shortage of construction workers in Puerto Rico. The volunteers are paid minimum wage for their time spent working and learning.

Website: https://www.protechos.org/
Email: info@protechos.org

Defensa Animal de Rincon, Inc.

Across Puerto Rico, thousands of cats, dogs, and horses suffer injury or illness from abuse and neglect or are starving on the streets. Defensa Animal de Rincon endeavors to save as many of these animals as possible, caring for and finding homes for unlucky animals. The organization covers necessary veterinary fees for sick and injured animals as well as sterilization or castration procedures.

Website: http://defensarincon.org/
Email: defensarincon@gmail.com

Save a Gato (SAG)

Save a Gato works to save the many abused or neglected stray gatos (cats) in Old San Juan by trapping them, sending them to the vet to be vaccinated, spayed, and de-wormed, and releasing them back into their original colonies, a process known as T/N/R (trap, neuter, release). Although Save a Gato is not a shelter due to a lack of space and resources, the organization does offer adoption for cats going through the T/N/R process. Those who don't find a home are released into their original colonies, which are monitored by volunteers to ensure the health of the cats.

Website: https://www.saveagato.com/
Email: saveagatopr@gmail.com

Love the Nations, Inc.

Unexpected pregnancies are a problem that plague women and families all around the world. Love the Nations offers 100% free services to support women who find themselves unexpectedly pregnant, including pregnancy tests, ultrasounds, domestic abuse care, doctor referrals, and more. The nonprofit also offers courses and education opportunities to teach mothers-to-be about parenting, relationships, and budgeting, among other topics.

Website: https://www.lovethenations.com/documents/
Email: joseph@lovethenations.com

Caribbean 12 Step, Inc.

Across Puerto Rico and the Caribbean, countless individuals are working through various 12-step programs to fight alcohol addiction and substance abuse and work toward a better future. Caribbean 12 Step, Inc. was formed to provide these individuals and their families with a safe and supportive environment and helpful services to facilitate their journey. The organization provides services in both English and Spanish.

Website: http://www.caribbean12step.org/home.html
Email: merribeth@caribbean12step.org

The Rain & Rose Charitable Fund, LLC

Over 40% of Puerto Rico's population lives below the poverty line, making the fight against poverty a major battle for various charities and nonprofit organizations. One such nonprofit is The Rain & Rose Charitable Fund, which is dedicated to providing Puerto Ricans with the tools and education they need to lift themselves out of poverty and propel themselves toward a brighter future.

Website: https://www.rainandrosefund.com/
Email: info@rainandrosefund.com

Rescate Playas Borinquen

Punta Borinquen is a rocky region in Puerto Rico's northwest, and Rescate Playas Borinquen's mission is to build up and preserve its natural beauty by picking up trash, mowing wild grass, and building trails and recreational areas, among other actions. The organization is dedicated to environmental protection and promotes recreational activities in the restored Punta Borinquen areas.

Website: http://rescateplayasborinquen.com/
Email: rescateplayasbqn@gmail.com

Museo de los Santos

Carved saints have been a tradition of Puerto Rico since the island was settled by Europeans. Museo de los Santos (Museum of the Saints) was originally founded in 1999 to provide information on Dr. José Torres Melendez's collection in English to tourists. Since then, the museum has grown significantly, to the point that it needed to be upgraded to a nonprofit corporation. The organization envisions becoming a self-sustaining museum, research institute, and exhibition space.

Website: http://museodelossantos.org/
Email: rholm@caribbeanconsulting.com

Karma Honey Project

Bees are arguably the most important insect on the planet, pollinating more than 70% of the crops the world needs for food. However, the bee population around the world has been rapidly declining in recent years. Karma Honey Project's mission is to revitalize the bee population in Puerto Rico through a variety of methods, including hosting beehives on local farmers' land and helping them sell the honey they produce locally, educating Puerto Rican children on the importance of bees, and rehoming misplaced bee colonies, thereby saving them from extermination.

Website: https://karmahoneyproject.com/
Email: karmahoneyproject@gmail.com

San Juan Community Library at Bucaplaa, Inc.

The benefits of reading are manifold for children and adults alike. The mission of the San Juan Community Library at Bucaplaa is to foster a love of reading within the community, as well as research and cultural enrichment. It is the only lending library in San Juan open to the general public.

Website: https://www.facebook.com/sanjuancommunitylibrary/
Email: c_estades@yahoo.com

Vitrina Solidaria, Inc.

Vitrina Solidaria (Solidarity Showcase) is a nonprofit dedicated to lifting up local sustainable and socially responsible Puerto Rican startups and small businesses, thereby promoting improved welfare locally across the island. The nonprofit helps small enterprises reach new markets by giving them the tools and education to succeed, particularly in digital marketing. In this way, Vitrina Solidaria enhances the wellbeing and prosperity of Puerto Rican communities while simultaneously boosting their local economies.

Website: http://www.vitrinasolidaria.org/
Email: info@vitrinasolidaria.org

Proyecto Esparciendo Amor

Proyecto Esparciendo Amor (Spreading Love Project) is a nonprofit organization whose mission is to help Puerto Rican youth and their families living in difficult situations. The entity focuses on youth in homes, shelters, and institutions with health conditions and/or mental or physical disabilities, as well as on youth and their families living in extreme poverty. It provides aid by covering benefactors' material needs or offering emotional support.

Website: https://www.facebook.com/pages/category/Nonprofit-
Organization/Proyecto-Esparciendo-AMOR-2128952600665334/
Email: proyectoesparciendoamor@gmail.com

ConPuerto Ricometidos

The primary mission of ConPuerto Ricometidos is to work toward a sustainable, stable, productive, and bright future in Puerto Rico, where residents have access to opportunities and enjoy a high quality of life. It works toward its mission by implementing development projects to rethink essential industries such as fishing and coffee-making, and it dedicates significant funds to rebuilding communities in the aftermath of disasters such as Hurricanes Irma and Maria in 2017 or the recent and ongoing earthquakes. It is also known for connecting Puerto Ricans on the island with Puerto Ricans living in the United States and other countries.

Website: https://www.conprmetidos.org/
Email: clay@conprmetidos.org

Boys & Girls Clubs of Puerto Rico, Inc.

Countless youth in Puerto Rico live in poverty. Children growing up in poverty miss out on important opportunities to gain a high-quality education and lift themselves up, thus reinforcing the cycle of poverty. The Boys & Girls Clubs of Puerto Rico works to empower in-need Puerto Rican youth to develop their skills and achieve their academic, professional, and personal goals. In this way, the nonprofit propels Puerto Rican youth toward a better and brighter future for themselves and the island.

Website: http://bgcpr.org/en/
Email: patricia.delatorre@bgcpr.org

Filing the Act 60 Annual Report

If you hold an Act 20, 22, or 60 decree, you will be required to file an annual report to the Department of Economic Development and Commerce (DDEC). The report is necessary to maintain compliance and remain in good standing with the DDEC. Note that this report is different from the annual LLC report—you will need to file both every year.

When to File the Report

The annual Act 60 report is due within 30 days of your income tax due date.

Report Fee and Requirements

Like with the annual LLC report, Act 20, 22, and 60 decree holders are required to submit a payment along with their file. Previously, all decrees incurred an annual fee of $300, but the fee for Act 22 and Act 60 investor Resident Individual decree holders was increased in 2021 to $5,000. All grantees must provide evidence that they complied with the conditions laid out in their respective grant during the tax year for which they are filing the report.

Let PRelocate Handle Your Report for You

If you fail to submit your annual report, you may incur administrative fines and even lose your decree, so compliance is crucial. However, we understand that you may have more important things to deal with as you operate your business. We would be happy to take this burden off your shoulders and file your annual report for you. We'll just ask you for some information, and that's all you have to do—we'll take care of the rest.

Information for Act 60 Individuals

Act 60 Overview for Individuals (Resident Investor Formerly Act 22)

On January 17, 2012, Puerto Rico enacted Act 22, known as the "Individual Investors Act." This Act was designed to help accelerate the economic recovery of Puerto Rico by attracting high net worth individuals, empty nesters, retirees, and investors to relocate to Puerto Rico.

In short, Act 22 provided 0% capital gains tax for gains you realized *after* moving to Puerto Rico, assuming you also satisfied calendar year bona fide residency requirements (as determined by the IRS). This is all possible because the Federal Government does not tax Puerto Rico residents, instead leaving that responsibility to the Puerto Rican government.

As of January 1, 2020, Act 22 has been replaced by Act 60, which brings with it some changes to the requirements.

There is a separate act for businesses called Act 20, which Act 60 has also replaced.

What Are the Tax Benefits for Act 60 - Individual Investor Act?

Eligible new Puerto Rico residents receive the following benefits for income accrued after the individual begins to become a bona fide resident of Puerto Rico before January 1, 2036:

1. 100% tax exemption from Puerto Rico income taxes on all dividends
2. 100% tax exemption from Puerto Rico income taxes on all interest
3. 100% tax exemption from Puerto Rico income taxes on all short-term and long-term capital gains
4. 100% tax exemption from Puerto Rico income taxes on all cryptocurrencies and other crypto assets

A few points of clarification:

1. Understanding the ins and outs of bona fide residency and the key dates associated with it are critical to your relocation and tax strategy. In the example of a stock, which is taxed as personal property and thus a capital gain, the date that establishes your tax basis is the date in which you commence becoming a bona fide resident; this is also known as your move date, or the date in which you cease to have a tax home in the United States. For Act 60 to kick in, you must successfully obtain your tax decree *and* satisfy the bona fide residency requirement for that calendar year (i.e., actually become a bona fide resident). If you do not accomplish these steps

in full, all income will be taxed in the United States (more on this in the next section).

2. Dividends and interest (benefits 1 and 2 above) are not considered capital gains, but rather "investment income," because the return is not reliant on the initial capital expenditure. For investment income, the IRS considers the source of income to be where the payer, or company, is located. Therefore, unless the payer is based in Puerto Rico, you will owe U.S. taxes on investment income even after moving to Puerto Rico. See our sources of income table at the bottom of this article for more information.

You Need to Actually Move to Puerto Rico

As part of Act 60 you need to become a bona fide resident of Puerto Rico. A bona fide resident of Puerto Rico is a person who can meet all three of the following IRS tests:

1. **Presence test**: The individual is present for at least 183 days during the taxable year in Puerto Rico (there are other ways to ways to satisfy this requirement). This is known as the "where are you" test.
2. **Tax home test**: The individual does not have a tax home outside of Puerto Rico during the taxable year. This is known as "the office test."
3. **Closer connection test**: The individual does not have a closer connection to the United States or a foreign country than to Puerto Rico. This is known as the "in your heart test."

These tests are explained in depth in the Act 60 Residency Requirements section.

One major change to Act 60 is the additional requirement to purchase property in Puerto Rico. The grantee must purchase real estate property in Puerto Rico within two years of obtaining the decree, and the property must remain the grantee's primary residence throughout the validity of the decree.

When Should You Actually Move to Puerto Rico?

There has long been confusion around which date you should use to establish your tax basis on a security when coming to Puerto Rico, which in turn determines your income tax obligation. Is it January 1 of the year you move? Or your move date? Or your Act 60 application or acceptance date? For capital gains and Act 60, the answer is based on the type of income and your residency status, which is mostly determined by the IRS and not Act 60. The Act 60 component is what then exempts you from Puerto Rico income tax (e.g., Puerto Rico capital gains).

34

Here's an example of a stock, which is taxed as personal property based on the owner's tax home:

1. Apply for Act 60 anytime during calendar year.
2. Move to Puerto Rico and take steps to establish residency.
3. Meet the Puerto Rico bona fide residency requirements during calendar year, which means you are a bona fide resident for that *entire* year. In general, this means you would need to move before July 1 to achieve 183+ days.
4. Prove residency when you accept your Act 60 decree, thus making it effective.

For personal property like a stock, your "move date to Puerto Rico" determines the date of sourcing because your tax liability is based on the residence of the taxpayer.

Now that you have your tax basis date established, you need to determine *how* to allocate the unrealized gain to each jurisdiction. We say unrealized because if you've already realized or closed the position prior to moving, this gain is not relevant for Puerto Rico.

What if You Have Previously Lived in Puerto Rico?

When Act 22 was initially enacted, grantees were required to have not lived in Puerto Rico for at least 15 years prior to the enactment of the law. This was amended to six years in 2017. Now, with Act 60, the period has been extended to 10 years before the Act's effective date. This means that to be eligible, the individual must have not lived in Puerto Rico since January 1, 2010.

What About Your Gains *Before* Moving to Puerto Rico?

Capital gains accrued before the individual established residency in Puerto Rico ("Non-Puerto Rican Built-in Gains") are subject to preferential Puerto Rican income tax rates:

- Within 10 years – if gain is recognized within 10 years of establishing residency in Puerto Rico, it will be taxed only at the U.S. federal income tax rate for capital gains.
- After 10 years – if gain is recognized after 10 years of establishing residency in Puerto Rico but before January 1, 2036, it will be taxed at a flat Puerto Rico tax of 5%, and the U.S. federal government will not pursue a capital gains tax.

Example 1 – Within 10 years

- A stock is acquired by a U.S. resident for $100 in 2013
- The stock is worth $200 in 2020, just before the U.S. resident moves to Puerto Rico
- The stock is sold by the now Puerto Rican resident in 2026 for $300

Cost: $100	U.S. Tax	Puerto Rico Tax
"Non-Puerto Rico Built-in Gains": $100 = $200 – $100	U.S. long-term cap gains (23.8%: $23.80)	0%
"Puerto Rico Gain": $100 = $300 – $200	N/A	0% Act 22

Example 2 – After 10 years

- Using the same scenario in Example 1
- The stock is instead sold by the now Puerto Rican resident in 2031 for $300

Cost: $100	U.S. Tax	Puerto Rico Tax
"Non-Puerto Rico Built-in Gains": $100 = $200 – $100	0%	P.R. special rate (5%: $5)
"Puerto Rico Gain": $100 = $300 – $200	N/A	0% Act 22

There Are Two Types of Securities You May Need to Establish a Tax Basis For:

1. Publicly traded security (marketable) – to determine the amount of "non-Puerto Rico built-in gains" versus "Puerto Rico built-in gains," the best practice is to take a snapshot of the asset price on the day you moved. You cannot import non-Puerto Rico built-in gains to Puerto Rico and treat those

gains as Puerto Rican-sourced income. You can only treat appreciation on publicly traded securities in excess of the amount in non-Puerto Rico built-in gains as Puerto Rican-sourced income.

2. Privately held business interest (non-marketable) – to determine the amount of "non-Puerto Rico built-in gains" versus "Puerto Rico built-in gains," the investor is responsible for setting the valuation. The investor would apportion the gain as either non-Puerto Rico or Puerto Rico based on the numbers of days the asset has been held in each location. In other words, this calculation is the percentage of all days the individual has held the asset as Puerto Rican-sourced income while living in Puerto Rico. For Private investments it is best to get high quality advice from a tax advisor on the proper way to treat these gains.

How Do You Get the Tax Exemption Decree?

The individual needs to submit an application to the Office of Industrial Tax Exemption (OITE) of Puerto Rico to obtain a tax exemption decree, which provides the full details of the tax rates and conditions mandated by the Act. This decree is considered a contract between the government of Puerto Rico and the individual investor. Once the individual investor obtains the tax exemption decree, the benefits granted are secured during the term of the decree, irrespective of any changes in the applicable Puerto Rico tax laws. The decree is initially valid for 15 years and can be extended for an additional 15 years.

How Much Does Act 60 (Individual) Cost?[1]

- Application filing fee: $750
- Acceptance filing fee: $50
- Additional sworn statement filing fees: ~$55
- Annual $10,000 donation to "nonprofit entities operating in Puerto Rico and are certified under Section 1101.01 of the Internal Revenue Code of Puerto Rico, which is not controlled by the same person who owns the decree nor by their descendants or ascendants"
- Annual report filing fee: $5,000

Where is Your Income Sourced From?

Determining where your income is sourced will dictate where you file a tax return. In determining whether Puerto Rico is right for you, and because tax rates vary, it is critical to know whether the United States or Puerto Rico has authority.

---

[1] Fees may have increased as of the printing of this book so readers can email us for the current fee schedule.

In general, the rules in the United States apply to all U.S. possessions, such as Puerto Rico.

General Rules for Determining U.S. Source of Income Source (IRS Table 2-1)

Item of Income	Factor Determining Source
Salaries, wages, and other compensation for labor or personal services	Where labor or services performed. If split between two locations, a time basis is applied.
Pensions	Contributions: Where services were performed that earned the pension Investment earnings. Where pension trust is located.
Investment income – Interest	Residence of payer
Investment income – Dividends	Where the paying corporation is created or organized
Investment income – Rents	Location of property
Royalties: Natural resources, patents, copyrights, etc.	Location of property where property is used
Sale of business inventory— purchased	Where items were sold
Sale of business inventory— produced	Allocation if produced and sold in different locations
Sale of real property	Location of property
Sale of personal property	Seller's tax home (See Special Rules for Gains from Dispositions of Certain Property for exceptions)
Sale of natural resources	Allocation based on fair market value of product at export terminal

Expat Tax Guide

The 2020 Guide to the Foreign Earned Income Exclusion for Expats

Tax season is always stressful, especially for expats, whose income is subject to double taxation. U.S. citizens on foreign soil pay income tax to the host country's government as well as to the IRS. Fortunately, the Foreign Earned Income Exclusion (FEIE) in the U.S. tax code allows expats to keep more of their money as long as they meet residence or presence requirements.

In 2021, the FEIE increased from the first $107,600 in foreign-earned income to $108,700. Since the exclusion is pegged to inflation, it's likely it will increase each year. It is important to note, however, that Puerto Rico is **not** a foreign country.

Qualifying Income

Only wages and self-employed earnings are eligible for FEIE. You may also be able to deduct foreign housing costs if they exceed 16% of the FEIE. In 2021, the maximum excludable housing amount is $17,392.

IRS guidelines exclude the following types of income:
- Salaries for civilian employees or military service members of the U.S. government
- Income earned for work in international waters
- Certain combat zone pay
- Housing, meal, and travel allowances paid by your employer
- Social Security, pension, and annuity payments

Keep in mind that these exclusions only lower your income tax liability, not any self-employment taxes you owe for Social Security and Medicare benefits.

Passing the Bona Fide Residence Test

You have to be a full-time resident of a foreign country for the full 12-month period of the tax year (January 1 through December 31) to qualify as a bona fide resident. Vacations, including short trips back to the United States, won't make you fail the residence test, as long as the trips were short and you clearly intended to return to your home in the foreign country.

One thing to keep in mind: If the host government has determined you are not a resident subject to its income tax laws, you can't use the FEIE regulation to lower your U.S. tax liability.

Passing the Physical Presence Test

To use the FEIE, you need to demonstrate that you are either a bona fide resident or were physically present in the country for at least 330 consecutive days in a single year.

The year doesn't have to be a calendar year—it can be any 12-month period you choose. A "day" for the purposes of the test is a full 24 hours, so your arrival and departure days in the country don't count.

If you choose a 12-month period that overlaps two different tax years, you can prorate the maximum exclusion and spread it out over the tax returns of those two years.

If there is war or civil unrest in the foreign country, you may apply for a waiver for the presence or resident test, but only if you can show that you would have stayed in the host country if those events hadn't occurred.

Understanding the Housing Exclusion

This exclusion only applies to employees earning wages in a foreign country, not for contract workers or other self-employed individuals, although those workers can still deduct actual housing expenses.

The FEIE and the housing exclusion can be combined, as long as the same income isn't counted in both exclusions. In other words, you should have an income of at least $122,664 between your wages and any housing allowances paid by your employer.

The following expenses generally qualify for the exclusion:
- Rent or fair-value rent for employer-provided housing
- Property and personal property insurance
- Utilities (minus personal phone service)
- Parking fees
- Furniture rental

You can't exclude things such as domestic services (maids, gardeners), mortgage principal and interest, or home improvements.

Comparing Act 60 and the Foreign Earned Income Exclusion

If you operate a business in a foreign country and use the FEIE to reduce your tax liability, it may be worth comparing the tax advantages of Puerto Rico's Act 60 for export services businesses. Eligible businesses pay a corporate tax rate of just 4%, and dividends are 100% tax exempt.

Act 60's Export Services tax incentive approaches income tax from the opposite perspective of the FEIE. In other words, you pay yourself a reasonable salary, and everything else is taxed at the 4% corporate rate. As a bona fide resident of Puerto Rico, you don't pay U.S. income tax on your salary, although you must pay Puerto Rican income tax on it.

With FEIE, you exclude the first $108,700 of foreign-earned income from your U.S. income tax and pay your regular rate on any earnings above that amount.

If you have a service-based business (consulting, creative services, professional services, data processing, call centers, import-export, or trading, for example), you may be surprised by the financial advantages available under Puerto Rico's Export Services Act.

Young Entrepreneurs Incentive Overview

The two well-known Puerto Rican tax incentives are Export Services (formerly Act 20) and Investor Resident Individual (formerly Act 22), but they aren't the only tax incentives Puerto Rico offers. There are various other tax incentives that aim to bring specific types of businesses to the island or, in the case of the Young Entrepreneurs, foster the talent already on the island. The Young Entrepreneurs tax incentive is open to any Puerto Rico resident between the ages of 16 and 35.

The Young Entrepreneurs tax incentive was formerly known as Act 135 before the introduction of Act 60 in 2019. While Act 135 offered, in addition to tax incentives for businesses, tax exemptions for salaries, services rendered, and self-employment income for young Puerto Rican professionals between 16 and 26, the revised Young Entrepreneur Act focuses only on businesses launched by young Puerto Rican entrepreneurs. The Puerto Rican government's intention with the act is to entice young professionals who have left Puerto Rico to return to their homeland and start a business under favorable startup conditions.

Benefits of the Young Entrepreneur Act:
- 0% fixed income tax rate (for the first $500,000)
- 100% tax exemption on property taxes
- 100% tax exemption on municipal taxes

Who Can Be a Young Entrepreneur?

The young and innovative contribute thousands of new businesses to the U.S. economy yearly. A 2012 study found that 26% of the new entrepreneurship activity in the United States was conducted by young entrepreneurs between the ages of 20 and 34. With the Young Entrepreneur tax incentive, Puerto Rico is endeavoring to bring more of that entrepreneurial spirit to the island.

To qualify, a young entrepreneur must be between 16 and 35 years of age and a bona fide resident of Puerto Rico. The entrepreneur must have a high school diploma or equivalent certification or be studying to obtain one. The entrepreneur's business must be an original, standalone venture that does not operate through an affiliated company. The company must be run specifically by young entrepreneur(s) only, and the entrepreneur(s) must intend to own and operate the long-term business indefinitely. To obtain the decree, the entrepreneur must apply for the incentives before launching the business and must sign a special agreement with the Secretary of the DDEC.

It is important to note that the Young Entrepreneur Act is valid for three years and is void if the entrepreneur receives a different tax incentive, such as the Export Services Act (formerly Act 20). Young entrepreneurs can receive the grant for a single business only.

Qualifying entrepreneurs require the following documents:
- Photo ID
- Original birth certificate
- High school diploma or equivalent certification, or a college degree
- Recent certification of No Tax Debt from the Treasury Department
- Tax return filing certification from the last five years with the Department of Finance
- Certificate of Incorporation, if applicable
- Recent Negative Real Property Certification of CRIM (with statement)
- Compliance Certifications Administration for Child Support

The Puerto Rico Startup Culture

A vibrant and energetic city, San Juan has become a hotspot for entrepreneurship in Puerto Rico. The city boasts numerous accelerator-type programs for entrepreneurs offered by groups such as Grupo Guyacán, StartUp Popular, and Parallel 18, providing Puerto Rican entrepreneurs with funding, investment, mentorship, and a unique place to work, among other benefits. The Young Entrepreneur Act is just a further incentive to launch a business in San Juan (or elsewhere in Puerto Rico), adding to the already favorable startup environment the island offers.

Individuals with Income from U.S. Possessions

On February 21, 2020, the IRS published an updated and revised Publication 570 – Tax Guide for Individuals With Income From U.S. Possessions (Publication 570). Publication 570 provides detailed information on the tax treatment for U.S. individuals with income sourced from U.S. possessions, including Puerto Rico. Publication 570 contains detailed rules and examples related to the IRS residency tests including information regarding determining days of presence days, closer connection, and tax home for U.S. individuals who may be considered bona fide residents of U.S. territories, including Puerto Rico. The most recent previous edition of Publication 570 was published February 22, 2019.

In the revised and updated Publication 570, the IRS has listed the following items below under the sub-heading "What's New."

What's New:

Disaster tax relief. In December 2019, disaster tax relief was enacted for those impacted by certain Presidentially declared disasters. Taxpayers in certain territories (see www.IRS.gov/DisasterTaxRelief) who are required to file a U.S. federal income tax return may be affected.

Automatic 60-day extension. Recent legislation provides an automatic 60-day extension of certain tax deadlines due to federally declared disasters that occur after December 20, 2019.

Form 1040-SR. Form 1040-SR, U.S. Tax Return for Seniors, has been introduced for 2019. You can use this form if you were born before January 2, 1955. The Form 1040-SR generally mirrors Form 1040. For more information, see Form 1040-SR and the Instructions for Forms 1040 and 1040-SR.

Qualified opportunity zones (QOZs). The Tax Cuts and Jobs Act (TCJA) amended the Internal Revenue Code to encourage investments in designated economically distressed communities by providing income tax benefits to taxpayers who invest new capital in businesses located within QOZs. There are QOZs located in the 50 states, the District of Columbia, American Samoa, the CNMI, Guam, Puerto Rico, and the USVI.

Bona fide residents of the CNMI, Guam, and the USVI will generally report qualifying investments on the income tax return they file with their territory tax agency, while residents of American Samoa and Puerto Rico will report qualifying investments on their U.S. income tax return. For additional information, see the QOZ FAQs at www.IRS.gov/newsroom/opportunity-zones-frequently-asked-questions. Taxpayers should also consult with their territory tax agency for additional information.

Standard deduction amount. For 2019, the standard deduction amount has increased for all filers.

Maximum income subject to social security tax. For 2021, the maximum amount of self-employment income subject to social security tax is $142,800.

Optional methods to figure net earnings. For 2021, the maximum income for using the optional methods is $5,880.

Other Tax Incentive Programs

Professional Physicians (Formerly Act 14)

To attract highly skilled medical professionals to the island, Puerto Rico is offering individual physicians who come to the territory to practice general medicine or any subfield of medicine tax incentives. Physicians completing their residency as part of an accredited medical program are also eligible. Physicians must complete at least 100 hours of work per month at a public or private hospital, federal or state agency, private office, or accredited medical school. Physicians may also qualify for exemption from the requirement to donate $10,000 to a nonprofit entity.

Eligible physicians can enjoy a 4% fixed income tax rate, and medical services businesses can enjoy a 100% exemption from withholding and paying income taxes on $250,000 per year.

Puerto Rico also offers a student loan repayment program for doctors, dentists, veterinarians, and medical researchers who graduated after July 1, 2019. To receive the $65,000 grant, applicants must remain in Puerto Rico for seven years, although interruptions to study additional medical programs outside of Puerto Rico are permitted.

Professional Researchers or Scientists (Formerly Act 14)

The Professional Researchers or Scientists Act endeavors to bring eligible researchers and scientists to the island to enrich its scientific and technological progress. Researchers and scientists contracted by the University of Puerto Rico or other authorized higher education institutes to engage in eligible scientific research are eligible for an income tax exemption on up to $195,000 in salaries received. Those contracted to engage in scientific and technological research and development services are eligible for an exemption on up to $250,000 in salaries received. To be eligible, researchers and scientists must complete 60 hours of community service per year.

Additionally, scientific researchers who earn or have earned a PhD after July 1, 2019 and agree to establish their services in Puerto Rico for a minimum of seven consecutive years may be eligible for a $65,000 subsidy issued at the beginning of the seven-year period.

Professional of Difficult Recruitment (Formerly Act 14)

Puerto Rico offers help in the form of tax incentives to businesses looking to hire difficult-to-recruit professionals whose specialized talents or skills are indispensable to the business. The position must be full-time, and the employee must be (or be willing to become) a resident of Puerto Rico and not benefit from the Investor Resident Individual decree (formerly Act 22). The business is exempt from wages and benefits paid to this employee above $100,000, but all income below this amount is subject to regular income tax. The professional is also exempt from the $10,000 nonprofit donation.

Creative Industries (Formerly Act 27)

One of Puerto Rico's objectives with Act 60 is to promote the island as a suitable location for film production and postproduction, as well as other creative projects. Thus, eligible creative projects can enjoy generous tax incentives in Puerto Rico. Eligible projects include films or short films, television dramas, reality TV shows, game shows, advertisement campaigns, video game projects, film festivals, and music videos. The final product must be primarily intended for consumption outside of Puerto Rico, although incidental consumption within Puerto Rico is permitted. For postproduction to qualify, the aggregate expenses must be at least $100,000. Strategic suppliers and infrastructure projects that facilitate film projects may also be eligible.

Tax incentives include:

- 4% fixed income tax rate
- 100% tax exemption on dividends
- 100% tax exemption on municipal taxes
- 75% tax exemption on property taxes
- 75% tax exemption on property under construction
- 100% tax exemption on gross capital gains
- 75% tax exemption on construction excise tax
- 100% tax exemption on excise tax and sales and use tax
- 100% tax exemption on rental income of movable property

Small and Medium Enterprises PYMES (Formerly Act 62)

To foster small and medium enterprises in Puerto Rico, the island is offering tax incentives to any natural person or entity operating or considering operating in Puerto Rico who has earned no more than $3,000,000 within the three-year period prior to applying and who has begun operating in Puerto Rico after July 1, 2019.

Tax advantages include:

- 100% tax exemption on property taxes for the first five years of the decree (subsequently 75%)
- 100% tax exemption on municipal taxes for the first five years of the decree (subsequently 50%)

47

- $1 yearly rent of an eligible DDEC property for the first three years of the lease
- Up to a 30% tax credit for the purchase of products manufactured in Puerto Rico

Manufacturing, Research, and Development (Formerly Act 73)

Puerto Rico is looking to encourage manufacturing, research and development, and high-tech industries to invest in the island, which is why it offers such companies generous tax incentives. Eligible businesses are ones that generate products using raw materials, including plant and animal matter. This definition is broad and even extends to businesses that engage in animal husbandry for research purposes, scientific research and development for new products, and select recycling activities.

Tax advantages include:

- 4% fixed income tax rate
- 100% tax exemption on dividends
- 50% tax exemption on municipal taxes
- 100% tax exemption on municipal taxes in the two semesters of business
- 75% tax exemption on property taxes
- 100% tax exemption on gross capital gains
- 100% tax exemption on construction excise tax
- 100% tax exemption on excise tax and sales and use tax
- 100% tax exemption on eligible investment income

Visiting Economy (Formerly Act 74)

One of Puerto Rico's objectives for its generous tax incentives is to foster the tourism industry in Puerto Rico and transform the island into a global-level tourist destination. To this end, the island offers tax exemptions to businesses engaging in eligible tourist activities. Among the eligible businesses are accommodation providers, such as hotels, guest houses, vacation clubs, and bed and breakfasts, as well as tourist attractions, such as casinos, theme parks, golf courses, and other entertainment venues that could promote tourism in Puerto Rico. Businesses that support medical tourism and nautical tourism are also included, as are e-sports leagues and businesses that develop and administrate natural resources such as caves, forests, and lakes.

Tax advantages include:

- 4% fixed income tax rate
- 100% tax exemption on dividends
- 50% tax exemption on municipal taxes
- 75% tax exemption on property taxes
- 100% tax exemption on property under construction
- 100% tax exemption on gross capital gains
- 100% tax exemption on municipal taxes in the first semester of business
- 75% tax exemption on construction excise tax
- 100% tax exemption on excise tax and sales and use tax
- 100% tax exemption on articles of use and consumption

Green Energy (Formerly Act 83-325)

Committed to promoting the green sector and preserving its natural beauty, Puerto Rico offers tax incentives to eligible green energy companies. Green energy companies are defined as entities that engage in the production of green energy; the production of highly efficient energy; the production, sale, or operation of highly efficient energy for consumption in Puerto Rico; equipment assembly and installation for highly efficient generation systems. Businesses requesting this decree are evaluated on various criteria, including paying employees more than the federal minimum wage, engaging in safe development, and using raw materials and agricultural products from Puerto Rico.

Tax advantages include:

- 4% fixed income tax rate
- 100% tax exemption on dividends
- 50% tax exemption on municipal taxes
- 100% tax exemption on municipal taxes in the two semesters of business
- 75% tax exemption on property taxes
- 100% tax exemption on property under construction
- 100% tax exemption on municipal tax for gross capital gains
- 75% tax exemption on construction excise tax
- 100% tax exemption on excise tax and sales and use tax
- 4% fixed income tax rate on the distribution, sale, or exchange of asset shares

Maritime Transport Services (Formerly Act 126)

Puerto Rico is looking to improve its economy and the welfare of its people by promoting maritime freight transportation between Puerto Rico and foreign nations. To this end, the island is offering tax incentives to businesses

49

established or to be established in Puerto Rico that engage in sea freight transportation between Puerto Rico and other countries or that derive income from the use, rental, or lease of a vessel or part used in such marine transportation. Businesses that engage in the repair, maintenance, or general conditioning of aircraft or maritime vessels may also be eligible.

Tax advantages include:

- 100% tax exemption on income tax
- 100% tax exemption on dividends
- 100% tax exemption on municipal taxes
- 100% tax exemption on movable and immovable property

Public Porters of Air Transport Services (Formerly Act 135)

Businesses who provide air transportation services as a public carrier may qualify for Puerto Rico's tax incentives. Businesses that engage in the repair, maintenance, or general conditioning of aircraft or maritime vessels may also be eligible.

Tax advantages include:

- 100% tax exemption on income tax
- 100% tax exemption on municipal taxes
- 100% tax exemption on movable and immovable property

Infrastructure Investment (Formerly Act 185-7)

In an effort to improve Puerto Rico's construction sector to foster its economic recovery and reconstruction, the island is offering eligible construction companies generous tax incentives. To qualify, companies must engage in the construction of buildings that will benefit the Puerto Rican economy and society. Eligible companies include those that improve, restore, or reconstruct existing buildings or construct new buildings in historical areas of Puerto Rico; construct or restore social interest housing for low- to moderate-income families; construct middle-class homes; construct, rent, or lease properties to senior citizens in a defined income bracket who do not own a home; and develop assisted housing for senior citizens.

Tax advantages include:

- 4% fixed income tax rate
- 100% tax exemption on property taxes
- 100% tax exemption on property under construction
- 90% tax exemption on municipal taxes

Agriculture, Livestock Industries, and Agribusiness (Formerly Act 225)

To strengthen its agriculture sector, Puerto Rico is offering tax incentives to businesses that engage in qualifying agricultural activities. Businesses that generate at least 51% of their gross income from the eligible agricultural activities can apply for the decree. Eligible agricultural activities include tilling or cultivating land for fruits, vegetables, or other useful plants; raising livestock for meat, eggs, or milk; commercial fishing activities; the commercial production of flowers for export (note that landscaping services do not qualify); and the rearing of thoroughbred racehorses and ride horses.

Tax advantages include:

- 90% tax exemption on bona fide farmers income tax
- 100% interest exemption on debt instruments
- 100% tax exemption on property taxes
- 100% tax exemption on municipal taxes
- 100% tax exemption on excise tax and sales and use tax.

Operating an Act 60 Business in Puerto Rico

Act 60 Business (Act 20 – Export Services) Overview

On January 17, 2012, Puerto Rico enacted Act 20, known as the "Export Services Act." This Act was designed to help accelerate the economic recovery of Puerto Rico by attracting new businesses and employment opportunities to Puerto Rico. Service businesses ranging from advertising to accounting to legal services, as well as hedge funds and a wide range of other consulting firms are eligible for the benefits.

In short, Act 20 provided a 4% corporate tax rate to businesses operating *inside* Puerto Rico, that receive income from customers located *outside* of Puerto Rico. This means a business needs to be able to remotely provide its services. This is all possible because the Federal Government does not tax Puerto Rico residents at the same rate at which it taxes residents of states.

As of January 1, 2020, Act 20 has been replaced by Act 60, which brings with it some changes to the requirements. In this guide, we outline the changes Act 60 has made to Act 20.

What are the tax benefits for Act 60 Puerto Rico?

Eligible businesses with operations *inside* Puerto Rico receive the following benefits for income derived from customers *outside* of Puerto Rico:

1. 4% corporate tax rate
2. 100% tax exemption on distributions from earnings and profits
3. 50% tax exemption on municipal taxes
4. 75% tax exemption on municipal and state property taxes (small and medium-sized businesses can receive a 100% exemption during their first five years of operation)

A few points of clarification:

1. "Operations inside Puerto Rico" is defined as work output or value created on Puerto Rico soil, whether that is by the business owner or employees.
2. The business owner and employees must receive a reasonable salary based on the services provided, which is taxed at ordinary Puerto Rico income tax rates (as high as 33%). This means you can't pass through 100% of net revenue at the 4% corporate tax rate.

3. In order to be eligible, businesses that generate an annual business volume of at least $3,000,000 must also directly employ at least one full-time employee. The employee must be a Puerto Rican resident and directly participate in the business activities pertinent to the decree.

Also note that under Act 60, the Office of Industrial Tax Exemption (OITE) will now execute independent audits of Act 60 businesses at least once every two years. These audits also apply to businesses that filed for Act 20 before Act 60 went into effect.

Which types of business are eligible for Act 60?

1. Research and development
2. Advertising and public relations
3. Consulting services, including, but not limited to, economic, scientific, environmental, technological, managerial, marketing, human resources, computer, and auditing consulting services
4. Advisory services on matters related to any industry or business
5. Creative industries
6. Production of blueprints, engineering and architectural services, and project management
7. Professional services such as legal, tax, and accounting services
8. Centralized managerial services, including, but not limited to, strategic direction, planning, and budgeting, provided by regional headquarters or a company engaged in the business of providing such services
9. Electronic data processing centers
10. Development of licensable computer software
11. Telecommunications voice and data between persons located outside of Puerto Rico
12. Call centers
13. Shared service centers
14. Storage and distribution centers
15. Educational and training services
16. Hospital and laboratories services, including telemedicine facilities and medical tourism services
17. Investment banking and other financial services, including, but not limited to, asset management, management of investment alternatives, management of activities related to private capital investment, management of coverage funds or high-risk funds, management of pools of capital, trust management that serves to convert different groups of assets into securities, and escrow account management services

18. Commercial and mercantile distribution of products manufactured in Puerto Rico for jurisdictions outside Puerto Rico
19. Assembly, bottling, and packaging operations of products for export
20. Trading companies
21. Blockchain-related services

The eligible business must not have a nexus with Puerto Rico. In other words, the services a business provides must not be related to the conduct of a trade, business, or other activity in Puerto Rico to qualify for the benefits of the Act. In general, this means the clients of the business need to be outside of Puerto Rico. The following services are considered to have a nexus with Puerto Rico, and are not eligible services:

1. Business or income-producing activities that are or have been performed in Puerto Rico by the applying business
2. The sale of any property for the use, consumption, or disposition in Puerto Rico
3. Counseling on the laws, regulations, and administrative determinations of the government of Puerto Rico and its instrumentalities
4. Lobbying on the laws, regulations, and administrative determinations of the government of Puerto Rico and its instrumentalities
5. Any other activity designated by the Secretary of the Department of Economic Development and Commerce of Puerto Rico

Is your business required to move to Puerto Rico?

Yes, the work needs to be performed in Puerto Rico to benefit from the tax advantages. There are two primary structures to accomplish this:

1. Act 60 businesses moving 100% of their income producing activities to Puerto Rico. In this scenario, you would set up a new entity in Puerto Rico, and then all value-producing employees would relocate to Puerto Rico (or be replaced). The U.S. business would then cease operations, and 100% of income would now be taxed from within Puerto Rico under Act 60.
2. Act 60 businesses moving a portion of their income producing activities to Puerto Rico. In this scenario, you would set up a new entity in Puerto Rico and then from that entity charge a "management fee" to your existing domestic eligible business. You would need a transfer pricing analysis and intercompany agreements to establish how much of your revenue you can appropriate to Puerto Rico resources vs. the existing U.S.

resources. This is required because the Puerto Rican company is a non-U.S. entity under U.S. tax law, and tax jurisdictions want to maximize their keep of tax revenues. Transfer pricing is a complex issue and we can provide guidance on the best strategy, accounting firms to work with, etc.

How do you get the tax exemption decree?

Your business needs to submit an application to the Office of Industrial Tax Exemption (OITE) of Puerto Rico to obtain a tax exemption decree, which provides the full details of the tax rates and conditions mandated by the Act and is considered a contract between the government of Puerto Rico and the business. Once the service provider obtains the tax exemption decree, the benefits granted are secured during the term of the decree, irrespective of any changes in the applicable Puerto Rico tax laws. The decree is initially valid for 15 years and can be extended for an additional 15 years.

PRelocate is a Qualified Promoter and will assist in your application at no cost (outside of actual expenses). Please reach out to us for more details.

How much does Act 60 cost?

- Application fee: $750
- Acceptance filing fee: $50[2]
- Additional sworn statements filings fees: ~$110
- Annual report filing fee: $500
- PRelocate support: Free if we are the Qualified Promoter and we assist in your move to Puerto Rico

---

[2] Fees may have increased as of the printing of this book so readers can email us for the current fee schedule.

The Benefits of Act 60 Export Services Tax Incentive

Do you run a business or are you planning to establish one? If your business satisfies the requirements, you may be eligible for the Act 60 Export Services tax incentive, as long as you relocate to or set up your business in Puerto Rico. The Export Services tax incentive is a powerful tax benefit that can save a young business considerable amounts of money, as it slashes your corporate tax rate to just 4%. This is significantly lower than the regular corporate tax rates of 37.5% in Puerto Rico and the U.S. federal corporate tax rate of 21%.

Businesses with an Act 60 Export Services decree also enjoy other benefits. In addition to the 4% corporate tax rate, Export Services businesses owe 0% on distributions from earnings and profits, save 50% on municipal taxes, and save 75% on municipal and state property taxes. If your business qualifies as a small or medium-sized business, it's completely exempt from municipal and state property taxes for your first five years of operation.

One caveat to bear in mind is that the business owner must be paid a "reasonable salary" based on the services they render, and this income is taxed at regular Puerto Rico income tax rates, which can be as high as 33%. Thus, it's not as simple as passing all your business revenue through the 4% corporate tax rate, but even with your salary, the savings you can amass through the Act 60 Export Services tax incentive are immense.

Requirements of Act 60 Export Services Businesses

How do you know whether your business qualifies for the Act 60 Export Services tax incentive? A hint lies in the name: export services. The idea behind the tax incentive is to stimulate the Puerto Rican economy and potentially generate new jobs for Puerto Rican workers, which means the business shouldn't negatively affect the Puerto Rican job market by taking away opportunities from other Puerto Rican businesses.

To be eligible for the tax incentive, a business must be located or established in Puerto Rico but provide remote services to clients located outside of Puerto Rico. The types of businesses that qualify are numerous—consultancy, accounting, tech, graphic design, and more—as long as the business renders its services to clients abroad and not in Puerto Rico, it may be eligible. Qualifying businesses are furthermore only eligible if they do not engage in certain activities, such as selling property for use in Puerto Rico or lobbying the Puerto Rican government.

If your business qualifies for the Act 60 Export Services tax incentive, consider relocating your business to Puerto Rico—you can save significantly on your taxes and help grow your business far more than under regular U.S. corporate tax rates. You may also consider relocating yourself to Puerto Rico under the Act 60 Investor Resident Individual tax incentive. Many of those who benefit from these tax incentives apply for both.

Corporate Filing Requirements

Puerto Rico's generous tax incentives can save you a lot of money, but unfortunately, they also entail a lot of bureaucracy. There are numerous corporate filings you must file regularly to remain in good standing with the Puerto Rican government. Here is a rundown of the reports you will be expected to file.

LLC Annual Report Filed with the Department of State

All LLC companies are required to submit an annual report to the Puerto Rican government, along with a $150 fee, to maintain good standing. Both the report and the fee are due each year by April 15. A two-month extension for a fee of $30 is possible, but the $150 fee must still be paid by April 15. Failure to pay on time will result in a $500 late fee and a 1.5% monthly interest rate.

Since Act 20/22/60 decree holders have a number of forms and reports to file, the schedule can become chaotic. PRelocate offers a service to file the annual report for Act 22 or Act 60 Investor Resident Individual businesses, lightening their load and freeing up more time for them to spend growing their business. You just provide some information about your business to us, and we will take care of the rest. For Act 20 or Act 60 Export Services companies, we can provide you with templates and information to dramatically facilitate the filing process. Additionally we have trusted tax and legal advisors to assist with all other aspects of the process.

Annual Report Filed with the Department of Economic Development and Commerce

Businesses that enjoy Puerto Rican tax incentives, such as Act 20 and Act 60 decree holders, are required to file an annual report along with the required filing fee for exempt businesses to the Office of Industrial Tax Exemption by the deadline established by law. Filing this report is crucial to maintaining your status as an Act 20/22/60 decree holder and failing to submit this report and the accompanying fee can result in the revocation of your decree. The filing process can be time-consuming and tiresome, but PRelocate is happy to offer our assistance.

For Act 22 and Act 60 Investor Resident Individual decree holders, there's also an additional step: proof of a $10,000 annual donation. More precisely, decree holders must make two separate donations of $5,000 in qualifying nonprofit organizations before December 31 of the relevant tax year.

59

Corporate Requirements

Act 20 and Act 60 business owners must also comply with numerous corporate requirements that all Puerto Rican businesses are subject to. We have provided a brief overview for you to familiarize yourself with. The list is non-exhaustive and should not be construed as legal or tax advice. We strongly recommend that all business owners work with a CPA to properly manage and file the below documents and any other business filings that may be required.

Annual

Informative Declaration and Reconciliation Statement of Income Tax Withholding

There are various forms businesses may have to file in relation to Puerto Rico's withholding tax requirements. Companies are required to submit forms for each individual who provided services worth more than $500 during the calendar year. The forms are due on February 28 each year.

Income Tax Return

Companies are required to file an annual income tax return every year by April 15. Businesses may apply for a three-month extension to file the return, but if they owe any Puerto Rican tax, they still must pay it by the April 15 deadline. If they fail to make the payment by the deadline, they will incur interest and penalties.

The typical corporate tax rate in Puerto Rico is 39%, but Act 20 and Act 60 Export Services businesses can enjoy a 4% tax rate.

Municipal Volume of Business Declaration/Patent Renewal

Businesses in Puerto Rico must obtain a municipal license to establish a business in a given municipality, and they are subject to annual municipal license taxes to maintain compliance. The rate varies depending on the municipality, but generally, it ranges between 0.2% and 0.5% of the overall gross revenue of the business. The municipal volume of business declaration must be filed by the fifth business day following April 15 of the given year, and the tax itself is to be paid in two installments on July 15 and January 15. Filing and paying the tax is not the same as renewing your business license—companies must renew their municipal license before the expiry date specified on it.

Personal Property Tax Return

Any entity that does business in Puerto Rico and who owns personal property used in said business on January 1 of each given year must pay personal property tax on that property. The rate varies from municipality to municipality but will not exceed 9.83% of the net book value of the property. Note, though, that Act 20 and Act 60 Export Services businesses are exempt from much of the property tax.

The return must be filed by May 15, although a three-month extension is possible. However, any personal property tax owed is due by May 15 of each year, regardless of extensions, unless the amount owed exceeds $1,000, in which case it is paid in installments on August 15, November 15, February 15, and May 15. If the amount is paid in installments, the business may enjoy a 5% discount.

Businesses who deposit the owed amount late incur late fees: 5% for payments later than 30 days, 10% for payments later than 60 days, and 15% for payments later than 90 days. Filing the return late will also result in a 5% monthly fee up to a maximum of 25%.

Workers' Compensation Insurance

Workers' compensation insurance is a mandatory insurance that provides indemnification for accidents that happen on the job or as a result of employment. Every single employee in a business, including the executive team, must be covered by this insurance.

The amount is paid by the employer only and varies depending on the type of business and the work performed. The annual report must be filed by July 20 each year, but the amount owed is paid in two installments, the dates for which are determined by the agency. In the report, the employer must indicate the number of employees at the business, the type of occupation of each, and the wages paid to each from the previous July 1 to June 30.

More information (in Spanish) can be found on fondopr.com.

Christmas Bonus

All companies in Puerto Rico must pay Christmas bonuses to any employee who has worked more than 1,350 hours during the period from October 1 to September 30 of the current year. The bonus must be paid by December 15.

The amount the employer must pay differs depending on the employee, the date they were hired, and how many hours they worked during the relevant period. If the bonus is $600 or less, the employer does not withhold taxes from it.

If, however, the amount is between $601 and $1,500, the employer is required to withhold 7% in taxes.

Businesses may request an extension for the payment if the total payment would exceed 15% of the business's total net income for the relevant period. They must request the extension by September 30. If the business fails to pay the bonuses by the deadline, employees are entitled to an additional 50% or 100%, depending on how late it is paid.

Monthly

Income Tax Withheld from Wages

Employers in Puerto Rico are subject to withholding a percentage of the wages they pay—typically 10% for Puerto Rican residents, although the percentage is higher for non-residents. Employers whose quarterly withholdings are between $500 and $50,000 are required to make monthly deposits by the 15th of the following month through the SURI portal. Employers whose quarterly withholdings are below $500 need only make quarterly deposits. The payment frequency an employer is subject to is determined by their payment history in the previous 12 months.

Income Tax Withheld from Professional Services

Like employers, businesses with independent contractors are also required to withhold 10% of wages paid for services rendered by independent contractors who are Puerto Rican residents. The amount increases to 29% for non-residents, although if the non-resident is a U.S. citizen, the amount is reduced to 20%. It is also worth noting that the first $500 paid to a given service provider in a calendar year is exempt. The associated form to file is Form 480.

The amount is to be deposited no later than the 10th day of the following month. The penalty for filing late or not at all is $500.

There are several exceptions to this withholding requirement, including services rendered outside of Puerto Rico or payments to Puerto Rican government agencies. A form for exempt or excluded income must be filed by February 28 of the following year.

Sales and Use Tax Monthly Return

Most merchants in Puerto Rico are required to charge 11.5% sales and use tax on items or services they sell. Most of this amount goes to the Commonwealth of Puerto Rico, with the small remainder going to the municipality. Monthly sales and use tax returns are due by the 20th of the following month electronically via the SURI portal. Additionally, all imports are also subject to the sales and use tax, and businesses that import items must file a monthly import return by the 10th of the following month.

Additionally, merchants must file a municipal sales and use tax monthly return. The tax rate varies from municipality to municipality, and Export Services businesses enjoy a 50% discount on municipal taxes.

Late filings that are less than 30 days late incur a 5% increase, with an additional 10% for each additional 30-day period until a maximum penalty amount of 25%.

Quarterly – Corporate Requirements

Employer's Annual Federal Unemployment Tax Return Form 940

Employers are required to pay 6% in Federal Unemployment Tax Act (FUTA) tax on the first $7,000 in wages paid to each employee per calendar year. Only employers are liable for this tax, so it must not be deducted from the employees' wages. The purpose of this tax is to provide unemployment compensation to workers who have lost their jobs.

Payments of this tax are due quarterly: April 30, July 31, October 31, and January 31. Failure to pay on time may result in late fees and interest.

Each January, employers are required to file Form 940 to report the total amount of unemployment taxes they paid in the previous year.

State Unemployment and Disability Insurance

To protect employees' income in the event that they are unable to work due to illness or a non-work-related injury, employers are required to pay a disability insurance tax on the first $9,000 paid to each employee in the calendar year. The amount to pay is 0.6%, and it is split evenly between the employer and the employee, with each paying 0.3%. Any additional compensation paid to the employee that exceeds the first $9,000 is not subject to this tax.

Payments of this tax are due quarterly: April 30, July 31, October 31, and January 31. Failure to pay on time may result in late fees and interest.

Social Security and Medicare

Employers in Puerto Rico must submit Social Security and Medicare payments for each employee. The total amount due for each employee is 15.3%, with the payment split evenly between the employer and employee at 7.65%

each. The employer withholds 7.65% and contributes an additional 7.65% from the gross salary. Of this money, 12.4% goes to OASDI, and 2.9% goes to Medicare.

Payments of this tax are due quarterly: April 30, July 31, October 31, and January 31. However, employers that owe more than $2,500 quarterly must make monthly payments by no later than the 15th of the next month. Failure to pay on time may result in late fees and interest.

LLC Compliance

The Importance of Maintaining LLC Compliance

Submitting reports—and especially paying the accompanying fees—is far from the most enjoyable part of running a company, but it is crucial that business owners maintain LLC compliance for their businesses. In Puerto Rico, all limited liability companies (LLCs), including Act 60 companies, are required to submit an annual report and pay a small fee to maintain good standing. Failure to comply with these regulations will result in administrative fines from the Secretary of State, so do not let this annual report slip your mind.

The annual report for the previous year is due on April 15 of each year and must be accompanied by a $150 fee. While it is possible (for a fee of $30) to apply for a two-month extension for the submission of the report itself, the $150 must be paid by April 15. Failure to pay the fee by April 15 will result in late fees to the tune of $500 plus 1.5% monthly interest.

What Information Is Needed for the Annual Report?

While corporations are required to submit detailed information, including a financial statement, LLCs have an easier workload: The information they must provide is more basic. This makes maintaining compliance much easier for LLCs.

Assistance Filing the Annual Report

While filing the mandatory annual report is significantly less complicated for LLCs than it is for corporations, it still eats up valuable time and energy you could be spending on more lucrative actions for your business. Furthermore, putting it off could be dangerous and could result in major financial ramifications.

For those interested in handing this task off to professionals and freeing up their minds to worry about other matters, we at PRelocate can handle this chore for you. Simply email us at info@relocatepuertorico.com to inquire about our annual report filing service. The process is simple: We will provide you with an Engagement Letter and a questionnaire to fill out, and we will handle everything else for you after that. If you are an existing client, we can even offer this service at a discounted rate.

Filing the annual report is crucial for LLCs but engaging the help of professionals can lighten your load. Whatever you do, just do not forget to file this report.

Opportunity Zone Designation

Puerto Rico Earns Opportunity Zone Designation

The Tax Cuts and Jobs Act of 2017 included a program to stimulate development in economically disadvantaged areas. Taxpayers who invested capital gains into projects in Qualified Opportunity Zones were eligible for tax incentives, including a reduction and deferment in capital gains taxes. The Opportunity Zones have now been approved, and 95% of Puerto Rico has been designated an Opportunity Zone.

In an attempt to further incentivize development in Puerto Rico, the Government of Puerto Rico enacted the Puerto Rico Economic Development Opportunity Zones Development Act on July 1, 2019. The bill establishes the regulatory framework for development in Opportunity Zones on the island, under the 2017 United States Tax Act.

"These zones are created to foster investment in the nation's disadvantaged communities. New investments in Opportunity Zones can receive preferential tax treatment, which will, in turn, be a boost to our economy," former Governor Ricardo Rosselló claimed.

What Act 21 Does

Quite simply, the Act 21 offers additional local tax incentives and makes a path for domestic taxpayers to take advantage of the tax benefits. Through a combination of tax credits and exemptions, the act increases the overall return on investment for development in Puerto Rico.

The Act 21 creates a "Priority Projects in Opportunity Zones Committee" made up of the Executive Director of the Puerto Rico Fiscal Agency and Financial Advisory Authority, the Public Chief Financial Officer, and the Public Chief Investment Officer. The committee will fall under the jurisdiction of the governor's office and is tasked with accepting and evaluating written proposals for development, and crafting rules and regulations for administering the program.

Under the terms of the Act 21, a Priority Project is defined as a business that is primarily focused on diversification, recovery, and economic and social improvement in a Qualified Opportunity Zone. Investors hoping to take advantage of the tax incentives and credits must submit a written proposal to the Committee identifying their eligible activities for approval.

Tax Incentives in Act 21

Once a project is approved by the Committee, it is eligible for an exemption lasting for a period of 15 years. There will be a flat income tax of 20% on income generated during the term of the exemption. Additionally, no tax or withholding will be applied to any dividend distributions resulting from earnings and revenue from eligible activities as defined by the committee.

Royalties paid to a non-resident party not engaged in the business will be subject to a 20% withholding tax.

For license and property taxes, an exemption of 50% will also be granted. If the Priority Project includes residential housing development, the exemption increases to 90%. Additionally, there will be no construction tax levied on Priority Projects. Interest income generated by financing Priority Projects engaged in eligible activities will also be exempt from income tax.

Finally, there is a 15% transferable tax credit on funds invested in exempted businesses, which can be sold to a third party. This credit will be given priority ranking over other tax credits available in Puerto Rico.

The Act amends Puerto Rico's tax code to align with the federal tax rules regarding Opportunity Zone projects. In other words, capital gains taxes will be deferred until 2026 to mirror current IRS rules, and there will be a 10% step-up in basis after five years, with an additional 5% step-up to a total of 15% on investments held for seven years.

The code allows new residents to defer capital gains taxes on earnings realized during the non-residency period.

Who is Eligible?

Any business seeking Priority Project approval must submit a proposal in writing to the Committee. If approval is granted, the business must file an exemption application with the Office of Industrial Tax Exemption.

Businesses currently receiving incentives under the Puerto Rico Film Industry Incentives Act, the Green Energy Incentives Act, the Export Services Act, the Tourism Development Act, or the Economic Incentives Act for the Development of Puerto Rico are not eligible for additional incentives under the Priority Project program.

Structuring a Qualified Zone Business

To begin, an investor must commit funds to a Qualified Opportunity Fund. A minimum of 90% of the assets from this fund must be invested in Qualified Opportunity Zone properties. These assets include:

- Tangible property acquired in 2018 or later which is used in the business or trade of a Qualified Opportunity business. Original use of the property must originate with the Qualified Opportunity Fund or, if acquired, the fund must substantially improve the property.
- Qualified Opportunity Zone stock is any domestic corporation operating as a Qualified Opportunity Zone business during most of its holding period; the stock must be procured in 2018 or later and paid for in cash (not cash equivalents or illiquid assets).
- Qualified Opportunity Zone partnerships mirror the terms and conditions placed upon Qualified Opportunity Zone stocks, but they are held in the form of a domestic partnership (instead of shares in a domestic corporation).

Any business whose assets are significantly composed of qualified opportunity zone properties is considered a qualified zone business.

Tax Deferred Benefits for Qualified Opportunity Zone Investors

Investments in Opportunity Zones earn deferrals on capital gains taxes. The deferral period ends at the time the investor sells its investment in the Qualified Opportunity Fund or December 31, 2026, whichever is earlier. The gain is calculated as follows:

1. Determine the cost basis of the investment (determined to be $0 initially).
2. Subtract the lesser of the excluded gain or the fair market value from the cost basis.
3. The difference is the capital gains that must be declared.

The cost basis of the investment, which starts out as zero, will increase (thus reducing potential capital gains) based upon the following timeline:

- If the investment is held for at least five years, the cost basis for the taxpayer will increase by 10% of the deferred gain. For example, if the deferred gain is estimated to be $1 million, the cost basis will increase by $100,000, or 10% of the $1 million deferred gain.
- If the investment is held for at least seven years, the taxpayer is granted an additional 5% increase in cost basis to 15% of the

deferred gain. Using the example above, the cost basis would increase to $150,000, or 15% of the $1 million deferred gain.

- If the investment is held for at least 10 years and extends beyond the December 31, 2026 maximum deferral date, the cost basis of the taxpayer's investment becomes equal to the fair market value of the investment, ending up with no capital gains to declare.

The best approach for a Qualified Opportunity Fund investor is to commit funds for at least one decade. Investors willing to risk funds in distressed communities for an extended period will be able to take full advantage of the tax savings that can accrue.

Opportunity Zone Map

Establishing a Business in Puerto Rico

What Permits Are Needed to Operate A Business in Puerto Rico

The type of permits a business needs depends on its industry, operation, and municipality. However, many companies need to apply for the following permits:

1. Permiso de Uso (Use Permit)
2. Certificación para la Prevención de Incendios (Fire Prevention Certificate)
3. Licencia Sanitaria (Sanitary License)
4. Exclusion Categorical (the Categorical Exclusion)
5. Certificación de Cumplimiento Ambiental por Exclusión Categórica (Certification of Environmental Compliance by Categorical Exclusion)

A full list of permits and corresponding manuals is available at the Single Business Portal, although the manuals are offered in Spanish only.

The Single Permit

Starting June 7, 2019, Puerto Rico's Permits Management Office of the Department of Economic Development and Commerce or Permits Management Office (OGPe by its Spanish acronym) combined numerous permits required to run a business on the island into a single permit fittingly called the Permiso Unico (Single Permit). The Single Permit consolidates the Use Permit, the Fire Prevention Certificate, the Sanitary License, and the Certification of Environmental Compliance by Categorical Exclusion, all of which are among the most common permits businesses need, into a single permit.

Prior to the introduction of the Single Business Permit, companies generally had to file for five to seven individual permits, depending on the type of business, in order to continue or commence operations. Now, eligible companies may only file a single application. The Single Business Permit is renewed each year.

Documents and Information Needed to Obtain Permits

Businesses are required to present a number of documents and pieces of information to obtain permits and certificates. The most common are listed below:

- Documentation from the corporation, including the registration, EIN, and Merchant Registry Certification
- A notarized property lease that indicates the exact square-foot area of the property
- Photographs of the property

- The tax number of the property
- A sketch of the property that includes the layout and dimensions
- A Municipal Business License or patent (businesses must register with the municipality in which they are located within six months of commencing operations)
- ABC Fire Extinguishers that undergo annual certification and are installed based on the square-foot area of the property
- Emergency signage and lights, including for the bathrooms (this need differs depending on the square-foot area of the property, its location, and the type of business)

The above is not an exhaustive list. Depending on the type of business you run, you may be required to submit additional documents or information. If you are unsure what permits are necessary for your business, it is a good idea to contact OGPe or an expeditor to discuss your business needs.

Save Time and Money with Our Virtual Mailbox Services

Applying for the necessary business permits, even the simplified Single Permit, is tedious and time-consuming. Your time and money can be put to better use focusing on your business. That is why we have implemented the Virtual Mailbox system. Using our system saves you precious time and removes the stress and hassle of applying for permits, keeping track of renewal dates, and worrying about inspections from OGPe. Our solution is affordable and will also save you money.

Services and Procedures Offered on the Single Business Portal

New Procedures on the Single Business Portal

In July 2018, Puerto Rico's Department of Economic Development and Commerce (abbreviated DDEC in Spanish) launched a new digital portal known as the Single Business Portal (SBP), which was meant to streamline the process of bureaucratic procedures, including setting up and managing a business in Puerto Rico. The system allows those setting up businesses on the island to apply for the necessary permits, licenses, certificates, and more simply and quickly from the online portal, eliminating the need for a trip to any government offices.

One of the system's goals is to attract investors to the Caribbean island territory by eliminating bureaucracy and facilitating the process of establishing a business in Puerto Rico. Economic Development Secretary Manuel Laboy also stated that the portal makes it possible to "measure the speed and effectiveness of the processes in a transparent manner," which has allowed the officials to tweak the development of the platform to improve the business environment and, ultimately, create more and better jobs across the island.

New Changes to the SBP

On October 2, 2019, after slightly more than a year in existence, the SBP was updated to include additional procedures, furthering the digitalization of the Puerto Rican business sector. From now on, the newly added procedures will be executed on the digital platform even if they were originally filed in person at the Office of Industrial Tax Exemption.

The following are the procedures that have been added:

- The filing of the following annual reports:

  - Act No. 8-1987 (Puerto Rico Tax Incentives Law) (under Law 8)
  - Act No. 135-1997 (Tax Incentives Act of 1998) (under Law 135)
  - Act No. 73-2008 (Puerto Rico Economic Incentives for Development Act) (under Law 73)
  - Act No. 83-2010 (Green Energy Incentives Act of Puerto Rico) (under Law 83)
  - Section 5023.04 of Act No. 1-2011 (Law 1 – Brewery)

- Notice of Residence Date (under Law 22)
- Notification of Commencement of Operations (under Laws 73, 83, and 20)
- Selection of Flexible Tax Exemption (under Laws 8, 135, 73, and 83)
- Opposition
- The following procedures related to laws administered by the Office of Industrial Tax Exemption:

  - Unconditional Acceptance of Decree and Amendments
  - Voluntary Delivery of Decree
  - Certification of Status of Request for Decree or Amendment
  - Certification of Compliance with Decree
  - Conversion of Decree

In addition to these new procedures, the SBP also now allows users to file amendments to annual reports (including the abovementioned) that they previously filed through the SBP. All payments are processed through the digital portal (additional processing fees apply).

Setting Up an Account

Users manage their affairs on the SBP through a Unique Profile, which they register for using their Social Security number, national identifier, or Employer Identification Number. Users can register as individuals, companies, or representatives of other individuals. From the Unique Profile, users can easily submit new applications and view the status and profile of existing applications. Users can also edit the information on their profile and add companies or individuals to it.

All in all, the Single Business Portal dramatically simplifies and expedites the bureaucratic processes required to set up a business in Puerto Rico and make the island an even more attractive destination for investors.

Hiring an Employee in Puerto Rico

How to Hire Employees in Puerto Rico

All over Puerto Rico are businesses that operate under Puerto Rico's Export Services tax incentive, formerly known as Act 20. Going forward, new Export Services businesses established under Act 60, will start to pop up rapidly. Since hiring at least one full-time Puerto Rican employee is a requirement for many of Puerto Rico's tax incentives, one of the most common questions Export Services decree holders have is how to hire employees in Puerto Rico.

Luckily for those looking to hire employees in Puerto Rico, the hiring practices are relatively similar to those in the United States, and Puerto Rico boasts a strong, vibrant workforce full of qualified workers for various positions.

Puerto Rico's Workforce

When the predecessor of the Puerto Rico Incentives Code, Act 20, was first introduced, the Puerto Rican government released a report to show prospective decree holders the many advantages of moving or establishing a business in Puerto Rico. The report highlighted Puerto Rico's workforce of 1.3 million, which includes a sizeable proportion of highly skilled workers. The 30,000+ decrees that Puerto Rico grants every year are clear evidence of the skills of the Puerto Rican workforce.

How to Recruit Employees in Puerto Rico

If you're looking to hire employees in Puerto Rico, check out the job bank maintained by the Puerto Rico Department of Labor. It's an entirely free service that allows you to create an employer account and sift through the resumes of potential employees.

Of course, the Internet is rife with other opportunities to find employees, as well. Many job banks that are popular in the United States, such as Indeed and Glassdoor, also have a strong presence in Puerto Rico, making them ideal recruitment platforms for Act 60 businesses. Social networks such as LinkedIn and Facebook can also serve as high-quality recruitment platforms. You can also try out Clasificados Online, Puerto Rico's own classifieds website, which, however poorly visually designed it is, is a fantastic way to hire employees in Puerto Rico.

Wages in Puerto Rico

One major bonus of hiring employees in Puerto Rico is the relatively low wages compared to the United States. According to Indeed statistics, here are the average wages for select jobs as of November 2021:

- Administrative assistant – $10.39 per hour
- Call center representative – $9.58 per hour
- Supervisor – $9.95 per hour
- Tutor – $16.21 per hour
- Home health aide – $12.39 per hour
- Programmer analyst – $20.37 per hour
- Software engineer – $19.89 per hour

Employee Benefits in Puerto Rico

Offering health and dental insurance benefits to employees is optional, but the Puerto Rican government has set various leave, wage, and hour requirements that all employers must adhere to.

Overtime

Any full-time employee who works more than 40 hours a week or 10 hours a day is entitled to overtime pay at one-and-a-half times their hourly wage. Any employee who works at least six hours a day has the right to a minimum 30-minute meal break.

Sick leave

Any employee who works at least 115 hours a month, which translates to 28 hours a week, or five and a half hours a day, is entitled to one day of sick leave per month. Companies with at least 15 employees must also allow workers to use sick time to care for family members, including parents, spouses, and children.

Paid time off

Any employee who works at least 130 hours a month is also entitled to paid vacation time. They accrue vacation days based on the amount of time they have worked for the company, as follows:

- 0.5 days per month the first year
- 0.75 days per month in the second through fifth years
- 1 day per month in the sixth through fifteenth years
- 1.25 days per month beyond the sixteenth year

You can find more information about Puerto Rico's hiring practices and labor laws at the Puerto Rico Department of Labor website.

Puerto Rico Payroll Taxes

Certain payroll taxes are applicable to any business that hires employees in Puerto Rico. They're generally similar to those in the United States, so if you've hired employees in the United States before, you may already be familiar with the general practices.

- **FICA taxes.** Puerto Rico employees are covered by Medicare and Social Security, so employers pay 7.65% in FICA taxes.

- **FUTA.** The unemployment tax rate is 0.6% on the first $7,000, after the 5.4% credit for the Puerto Rico unemployment tax.

- **Puerto Rico unemployment tax.** You pay 5.6% of the first $7,000 for each employee.

- **Disability tax.** This tax is shared equally between employer and employee and amounts to 0.6% of the first $9,000 in salary.

- **Worker's compensation insurance.** This tax is based on the type of work the employee performs.

Do I Have to Hire Employees in Puerto Rico under Act 60?

When Act 20 was originally passed, Puerto Rico's unemployment rate was nearly 18%, so the legislation included a provision that Act 20 businesses employ at least five employees in Puerto Rico, one of which could be the business owner. Later, after Puerto Rico's economy improved and the unemployment rate sank, the employee requirement was dropped.

Things changed again when Act 20 was replaced by Act 60. Act 60 brought a new employee requirement: Exempt businesses that generate at least $3,000,000 in annual revenue must directly employ at least one full-time employee. The employee has to be a bona fide resident of Puerto Rico who directly contributes to the business activities covered by the decree.

All in all, even if you have to hire employees in Puerto Rico, the process is relatively simple and straightforward. You can take advantage of a highly skilled labor force that works for significantly lower wages than in the United States while enjoying Puerto Rico's generous tax incentives.

Hiring Independent Contractors

The Withholding Requirements for Independent Contractors

In general, companies or individuals in Puerto Rico paying for services rendered must withhold a certain percentage of the amount paid for tax purposes, as stipulated by a December 10, 2018 amendment to Section 1062.03 of the Puerto Rico Internal Revenue Code of 2011. Effective January 1, 2019, individuals and corporations paying for services rendered are obligated to deduct and withhold income tax. However, the exact requirements and specifications differ dramatically for employees and independent contractors, and numerous categories of businesses are exempt. For employees, the situation is more in depth, with the payer required to withhold income tax, Social Security, and any other benefits that may be applicable. For independent contractors, the key requirement is to withhold 10% of the amount paid and send it to the Puerto Rico Treasury Department (Hacienda) through the SURI portal monthly.

Exemptions

Not every payment for services rendered is subject to the withholding requirement. Notably, the first $500 per calendar year paid to a given service provider is exempt.

However, there are other payments that are entirely exempt from the requirement, even if the payment exceeds $500 in a given year:

- Payments to hospitals, clinics, homes for the elderly, and institutions for the disabled (if a laboratory is an integral part of a hospital or clinic, it is also exempt)
- Payments to bona fide farmers
- Payments to contractors or subcontractors rendering construction services (note that architectural, engineering, design, consulting, and similar services are not exempt)
- Payments to the Puerto Rican government, including its agencies, public corporations, and political subdivisions
- Payments for church services
- Payments to nonprofit organizations certified by Hacienda
- Commission payments to direct salespeople of consumer products
- Payments of salaries and wages subject to withholding under Section 1062.01 of the 2011 Internal Revenue Code of Puerto Rico
- Payments to air or maritime carriers or entities providing telecommunication services between Puerto Rico and another region (any payments made by such entities to nonprofits for

services such as bookkeeping or reporting the sales of air or maritime tickets are also exempt)
- Payments for insurance contracting
- Payments for printing, for television or radio broadcasts, or to newspapers, magazines, or other publications, including for ad placement
- Payments (lease or sale) for personal or real estate property
- Payments to foreign entities not involved in trade or business with Puerto Rico
- Payments for services rendered outside of Puerto Rico

If the payment includes fees for additional activities, such as travel or machinery, the payer should request that the service provider separate the amounts on the bill to facilitate the calculation of the withholding amount.

Payments to Non-Puerto Rican Residents

If a payer makes a payment to a non-resident service renderer who is providing services in Puerto Rico without being registered in the Puerto Rico State Department to engage in trade or business in Puerto Rico, the payer must withhold 29% instead of the normal 10%. This percentage is reduced to 20% if the non-resident is a U.S. citizen.

As mentioned in the list above, payments for services rendered outside of Puerto Rico are not subject to the withholding requirement, but the payer must apply the B2B tax of 4%. Certain companies are exempt from this requirement.

Payer Responsibilities and Penalties

Payers are required to file the withholding amounts to Hacienda within the first 15 days of the month following the month during which the payment was made. Payers must also file quarterly and annual returns as well as informative declarations for payments not only for all services received but also for rent, advertising, insurance, telecommunications, and Internet and television access.

Payers incur a penalty of $500 for each informative declaration filed late or not at all. If they do not file an informative declaration, they are also unable to deduct the relevant expenses on their tax return.

Full Exemptions

A 100% exemption from the withholding requirement is available to new businesses. A new business is defined as an individual or entity that is in its first year of service and began operations (in or outside of Puerto Rico) during the calendar year for which it is requesting the exemption.

Individuals or corporations requesting this waiver must meet a series of requirements, including a Merchant Certificate, the authorization to do business in Puerto Rico, an Employer Identification Number, and the submission of previously filed tax returns. Individuals must also fill out an affidavit form (Form SC 2678) and prove that they have no debt with Hacienda, have not had any previous business, and are in their first year of rendering services. The additional requirements for corporations are a completed Model SC 2680 to request a Withholding Waiver Certificate and proof that the company owner has not previously rendered the same kind of services.

Partial Exemptions

Corporations that meet certain requirements are eligible for a 6% reduction of the withholding requirement. To be eligible, a corporation or partnership must have filed all income tax returns, have no outstanding debts with Hacienda (or have an approved payment plan for any outstanding debts), have forwarded the amount of net loss in operations, and prove that the withholding will lead to a tax refund or credit.

The exemption renews annually, with Hacienda automatically issuing a certificate through SURI to corporations that meet the requirements. Those who do not receive a certificate can request one at the closest District Collection Office.

Whether a business is fully or partially exempt, it must fill out and submit form SC 2755 for the respective year in order to enjoy the benefits of exemption.

Informative Declarations

By February 28 of the year following the payments, in addition to informative declarations, payers must file an Annual Reconciliation Return for the amounts withheld from Puerto Rico residents. For payments made to non-residents, the Annual Reconciliation Return is due by April 15 of the year following the payments.

Payers must also complete and send a copy of informative declaration forms 480.6A or 460.6B to each nonexempt entity to whom they paid more than $500 in the relevant calendar year. The informative declaration must also include the number of the total or partial waiver assigned to the entity who received payments. If the entity is subject to a full or partial waiver, the relevant number must also be included.

GILTI Tax

What the GILTI Tax Changes

The GILTI—or Global Intangible Low-Taxed Income—tax was enacted by the Trump administration and targets U.S. companies that operate controlled foreign companies (CFCs) for tax purposes. U.S. business owners who run a Puerto Rican-incorporated company from the United States fall into this category, so naturally, all non-resident export services tax decree holders are subject to this new tax.

Under GILTI regulations, all US-owned CFCs are subject to a minimum corporate tax rate of 10.5%. This means that non-resident export services tax decree holders currently enjoying the 4% corporate tax rate must pay additional taxes to the IRS. A rate of 10.5% is still significantly lower than the standard U.S. corporate tax rate of 39%, so you can still enjoy lowered tax rates without moving out of the United States. Please remember to qualify for the 4% tax rate the service has to be provided from Puerto Rico, so the business does have to physically operate and create the value in Puerto Rico.

In light of the GILTI tax, now only companies whose majority owner is a Puerto Rican resident can continue paying the low 4% rate. So, if you want to save that extra 6.5%, there's only one option: become a Puerto Rican resident.

We would recommend speaking with a CPA to be certain on your break-even, before pursuing the Puerto Rico-based route.

The Requirements to Become a Puerto Rican Resident

There are three key requirements you have to meet to be considered a bona fide Puerto Rico resident. If you fail to meet even just one of the three, you will not be legally considered a Puerto Rico resident. PRelocate offers a detailed residency guide to help you navigate the process.

Spend Most of Your Time in Puerto Rico

It is not enough to simply purchase a home in Puerto Rico. You must truly move your life to Puerto Rico and convince the Puerto Rican government that the island is your primary home. This means spending at least 183 days a year in Puerto Rico.

You can spend the other 182 days of the year anywhere in the world. You can spend time in other homes or jump from place to place nomadically, but you must always return to Puerto Rico, and if you own homes elsewhere, you must prove to the Puerto Rican government that your Puerto Rican home is the most significant one. It is not advised to spend 183 days in your Puerto Rican home and the remaining 182 in another home located off the island, since your non-Puerto Rican life will then seem as significant as your Puerto Rican life, and the government will not be convinced.

Make Puerto Rico Your Tax Home

Your tax home is the center of your economic activity—in other words, your office. In order to continue benefiting from the export services tax incentive under the GILTI tax, you have to move your office to Puerto Rico. You can still own and operate bank accounts in the United States, but it is not recommended to conduct all your financial activity through your U.S. accounts, as this will not help convince the Puerto Rican government that Puerto Rico is your tax home. The more economic ties to Puerto Rico you can demonstrate, the better, so it is recommended to make heavy use of your Puerto Rican bank account.

Prove That You Don't Have Closer Connections Elsewhere

There are various ways that you can persuade the Puerto Rican government that you don't have closer connections anywhere else. Moving yourself and your family into a permanent home on the island is just one factor (it will not be so convincing if you don't move your family). Move significant personal belongings to your new Puerto Rican home, as well.

You should also become part of your local Puerto Rican community, befriending locals and making professional contacts.

Establish your ties on paper, too. Obtain a Puerto Rican driver's license, list Puerto Rico as your official country of residence on documents and forms, and register to vote (and actually vote) in Puerto Rico.

Fill Out the Necessary Forms

Moving to another territory always involves paperwork, and relocating to Puerto Rico is no exception. If you begin or end bona fide residence in Puerto Rico, you are obligated to fill out the IRS Form 8898 – Statement for Individuals Who Begin or End Bona Fide Residence in a U.S. Possession. Alternatively, you can file IRS Form 8822 – Change of Address.

Do Not Cut Corners

Some people try to cut corners and trick the Puerto Rican and U.S. governments into believing they are bona fide Puerto Rican residents, but this can end up being a costly endeavor. Either commit fully to your new life in Puerto

Rico, or pay the extra taxes to the IRS to continue enjoying your life in the United States.

Transfer Pricing for Individual Businesses

Individuals with shared ownership in more than one business in different tax jurisdictions must consider transfer pricing, the study of how these businesses transact with each other. While the business owner desires to realize income and profits in the lowest tax jurisdiction, the opposing tax jurisdiction desires the opposite. Due to this possible conflict of interest the IRS has robust rules and methodologies in place to ensure that an appropriate transfer price, or allocation of value, has been established. The question any business needs to ask is, "if these two entities were not related, would the price being charged be reasonable and fair?" Transfer pricing is relevant for Act 60 companies that create value in both Puerto Rico and the United States.

> "Globalization and the rapid growth of international trade has made inter-company pricing an everyday necessity for the vast majority of businesses. However, the growth of national treasury deficits and the frequent use of the phrase 'transfer pricing' in the same sentence as 'tax shelters' and 'tax evasion' on the business pages of newspapers around the world have left multinational enterprises at the center of a storm of controversy."
>
> -PWC Transfer Pricing Report 2016

How Does Transfer Pricing Work?

The purpose of transfer pricing is to establish "arm's length" interactions, which requires prices charged between related parties be equivalent to those that would have been charged between independent parties in the same circumstances. Let's look at two simple examples:

Example 1: Tangible property (goods)

- PenCo U.S. manufactures a pen in the United States for $0.10.
- PenCo Puerto Rico sells the pen for $1.00 in Puerto Rico and spends $0.10 on marketing.
- PenCo US now has $0.80 of profits ($1.00 – $0.10 – $0.10).
- The transfer pricing question: Where does PenCo U.S. realize these profits, and in what amount? A number of variables will be taken into consideration to determine what percentage of the $0.80 gets assigned to Puerto Rico versus the United States. This in turn determines the tax obligation.

Example 2: Intangible property (services)

- BloodCo U.S. owns blood centers in Florida where they take blood from customers and earn $100.

- BloodCo Puerto Rico is based in Puerto Rico and manages the operations of BloodCo U.S.
- BloodCo Puerto Rico handles all executive leadership, strategy, expansion, and marketing from Puerto Rico.
- BloodCo Puerto Rico charges BloodCo U.S. a 75% "management fee" on all profits.
- The transfer price question: What percent of value is actually being created by BloodCo Puerto Rico? Is this 75% reasonable? This allocation will determine the tax obligation.

What is a Transfer Pricing Study?

A company completes a transfer pricing study to provide the economic analysis necessary to support its transfer pricing decisions in case it is challenged by the IRS or tax authorities in another jurisdiction.

Transfer pricing is closely monitored within a company's financial reporting and can become even more important when requested by regulators or auditors. If inappropriately documented, a business can incur material taxes, fees, or penalties. While companies like Apple grab the headlines for their various shell companies around the world, all businesses should be on the offensive to ensure compliance.

Considerations for a transfer pricing study:

- Analysis of value creation
- Economic circumstances
- Market analysis to establish a non-related entity basis
- Inter-company agreements for each transaction or transfer
- Annual reviews
- Audit readiness
- Compliance with IRS Section 482

Outputs of a transfer pricing study:

- A transfer pricing policy
- Documentation of company structure and transactions
- Decision rationale
- Conclusions that establish said transfer prices are reasonable

Transfer Pricing Considerations as They Relate to Puerto Rico

There is no absolute rule for determining a transfer price, which leaves companies exposed to tax authorities and operating with a degree of uncertainty. At a minimum, a company will want to have documentation and evidence that describes an approach before doing business so that you can produce it quickly in the event of an audit. Case law is rife with examples of businesses that failed to consider transfer pricing—the penalties and costs can be severe. Businesses with substantial operations in the United States are encouraged to consider commissioning a transfer pricing study.

Moving to Puerto Rico

Pre-Move Checklist

Puerto Rico Relocation Checklist: What to Do Before Your Move

There are many processes you have to undertake before you make the move. Use the following information as a checklist to make sure you do not forget any essential moving procedures.

Gather Your Birth Certificate and Social Security Card

Make sure you have your birth certificate and Social Security card ready, because you will need them to complete various procedures. Your Social Security card is necessary to apply for the Individual Resident Investor tax grant and to put utilities in your name. You will also need to make sure they are originals—copies will not suffice. Once you have your birth certificate and Social Security card, you can start with the more involved procedures.

Request a Background Check From Your State

Puerto Rico wants to make sure you are not a criminal before you set off to reside on its shores, so requesting a criminal background check from your state is a must. The procedure varies from state to state, so be sure to read up on the requirements for your particular state. Notably, some states, such as California, New York, and Oregon, require fingerprinting, while others, such as Florida, Texas, and Michigan, do not. For the states that require fingerprinting, the background check typically takes longer, and you may have to wait a while to receive the results. Please reach out to us at info@relocatepuertorico.com for a list of the states that require fingerprinting.

Request an Official Copy of Your State Driving Record

In order to apply for a Puerto Rican driver's license, you need to present a copy of your state driving record, and the easiest course of action is to obtain the record before you move. You can simply request a driving record at your local DMV or online for a small fee, which varies from state to state. You'll need to present it at your local Driver Services Center (CESCO) in Puerto Rico to get your Puerto Rican driver's license.

Apply for a Puerto Rican Driver's License

Getting a Puerto Rican driver's license is recommended to help satisfy the closer connections test and prove bona fide residency in Puerto Rico. The process can be somewhat complicated, so check out our comprehensive guide for how to get a Puerto Rican driver's license. You will be required to surrender your U.S. driver's license, as you are not allowed to have two different licenses.

Give Up Your U.S. Voter Registration

After you arrive on the island, make sure to give up your U.S. voter registration, as you will not be allowed to vote in U.S. elections as a Puerto Rican resident. Giving up your right to vote in U.S. elections and assuming the right to vote in Puerto Rico elections can also help you pass the closer connection test to prove bona fide residency in Puerto Rico. Download and use the Election Directory for Cancellation Notices to determine the address to send your cancellation notice to.

Submit a Declaration of Non-Domicile

Finally, when you have a Puerto Rican address and have settled into your new home, submit a declaration of non-domicile to the Office of the Clerk in your current state of domicile. The declaration of non-domicile is necessary to cancel your domicile in your previous state and, depending on the state, void your income tax status there. Declaring non-domicile is also necessary to declare domicile in Puerto Rico, which you should do to indicate your intention to reside on the island long-term. Templates for both declarations are available for download on our website blog.

Other Recommended Steps for Relocating to Puerto Rico

We have already covered all the key bureaucratic procedures you need to complete for your move to Puerto Rico, but there are a number of other procedures we strongly recommend to prepare for your new Caribbean life.

Get a Medical Checkup in the United States

Once you are in Puerto Rico, you will have to switch your medical insurance and find a new doctor, so it is wise to get all your checkups out of the way while you are still in the United States.

Join the Act 20/22 Resource Group on Facebook

Some of the best sources of information on relocation to Puerto Rico are the people who have already gone through the process themselves. In the "Puerto Rico Act 20/22 – Resource Group" on Facebook, members can communicate with others who have already moved to Puerto Rico under Act 20 or 22 or are in the process of doing so under Act 60. The community is large and friendly, and members post polls and referrals as well as share events.

Brush Up on Your Spanish

Most Puerto Ricans can communicate in English, but they are still more comfortable with Spanish, and a working knowledge of Spanish can go a long way in Puerto Rico. If you can speak Spanish, you will have a leg up in official procedures and business matters, and it will allow you to develop deeper connections with the locals in your community.

While you could enroll in a class, it is often more effective to study independently, which you can do for free with resources like Duolingo. If you prefer the guidance of a teacher, private lessons, such as on italki, are more effective than group classes. From roughly an intermediate level, it is highly recommended that you watch Spanish movies, read Spanish books, and do other activities in Spanish to enhance your language skills.

Sell or Rent Your Home in the United States

The Puerto Rican government wants to be sure that you intend to reside long-term in Puerto Rico, in which case you certainly do not need a house in the United States. If you keep your U.S. home without renting it, the government may fear that you are not as committed to Puerto Rico as you claim, making it more difficult to satisfy the closer connections test. Additionally, selling or renting your home will give you some extra cash to help fund your new life in Puerto Rico or to invest in your business.

Research Puerto Rican Locations

Since you will be moving your entire life to Puerto Rico, including your family, it is important to consider the location to which you are moving. Puerto Rico features many unique areas, so whether you are looking for a family-friendly neighborhood, a cozy beachside town, or a place with a lively nightlife scene, if you do your research, you are bound to find the right Puerto Rican neighborhood for you.

Research Puerto Rico Schools

If you have school-aged children, schools will also be an important consideration in your move to Puerto Rico. The island features an array of international schools where children are taught in English, although enrollment in regular Spanish-speaking schools is also possible if your children have the necessary language skills. As an alternative, you can look into homeschooling options.

Throw a Going-Away Party

While your move to Puerto Rico is exciting, don't get so caught up in moving procedures that you forget to spend quality time with your loved ones. Throwing a going-away party before your move is a good way to say goodbye to the people in your life in the United States and close that chapter of your life before opening a new one in Puerto Rico.

Puerto Rico Citizenship

How to Obtain A Puerto Rican Citizenship Certificate

In most cases, taking on citizenship in a new jurisdiction is a long and complicated process that requires years of permanent residency in the new territory. For U.S. citizens, Puerto Rico is an exception: given that Puerto Rico is a U.S. territory, Puerto Ricans are already U.S. citizens by birth. Thus, when mainland U.S. citizens wish to obtain a Puerto Rican citizenship certificate, they aren't actually undergoing another country's naturalization process. This makes the process relatively quick and easy with fairly relaxed application criteria, so any Act 20/22/60 decree holder is encouraged to obtain a Puerto Rican citizenship certificate.

Why Apply for a Puerto Rican Citizenship Certificate?

Since U.S. citizens can reside in Puerto Rico indefinitely, you may question why you should bother applying for a Puerto Rican citizenship certificate. Indeed, it's not obligatory, and Act 20/22/60 holders can continue to enjoy the lucrative tax benefits Puerto Rico offers without obtaining a Puerto Rican citizenship certificate.

However, to maintain compliance and reap the benefits of the tax exemptions, Act 22 and Act 60 Investor Resident Individual decree holders must pass Puerto Rico's bona fide residency tests annually, and having a Puerto Rican citizenship certificate can help. The most subjective and, for some, the most difficult of the three residency tests is the closer connection test, which evaluates whether a decree holder maintains closer ties to Puerto Rico or the mainland United States. Obtaining a Puerto Rican citizenship certificate indicates one's loyalty to Puerto Rico and intention to reside on the island long term, meaning it serves as reinforcement of one's ties to Puerto Rico.

Besides, applying for a Puerto Rican citizenship certificate is quick and easy and only costs $30, so there's hardly any reason not to do it. The proof of ties to Puerto Rico can be invaluable for the closer connection test, and having a Puerto Rican citizenship certificate can help you feel closer and more connected to your new island home.

How to Apply for a Puerto Rican Citizenship Certificate

To be eligible to apply for a Puerto Rican citizenship certificate, you must either:

- Have been born in Puerto Rico
- Have U.S. citizenship and at least one parent who was born in Puerto Rico
- Have U.S. citizenship and have resided in Puerto Rico for at least one year before applying
- Have been declared a citizen of Puerto Rico by a competent court of law

Most Act 20/22/60 decree holders seeking a Puerto Rican citizenship certificate are likely to fall into the third category, which means they require documentation to prove they have lived in Puerto Rico for at least one year. The Puerto Rican government accepts the following documents as proof:

- Invoices for water, electricity, and internet/phone services for 12 months at the address indicated in the application
- A valid Puerto Rican driver's license or other piece of identification with a photo and signature issued by the Puerto Rican government
- An employment certificate, payroll stub, or other proof of employment in Puerto Rico over the preceding 12 months
- A copy of the first page of your most recently filed income tax return

To obtain a Puerto Rican citizenship certificate, you must submit a request in writing using the PDF form provided by the island's government. It must be accompanied with $30 in IRS stamps (*comprobante*), your original birth certificate, and photo ID. The application process is that simple—afterward, you'll receive a Puerto Rican citizenship certificate to strengthen your standing in the closer connection test.

Renewing Your Passport in Puerto Rico

Since Puerto Rico is a U.S. territory, its citizens hold U.S. passports, which means you don't need a passport to move to Puerto Rico under Act 60. If you have one, though, Puerto Rico's status also makes renewing your U.S. passport in Puerto Rico fairly simple. If you are a U.S. citizen, you can easily renew your passport in Puerto Rico as long as it is undamaged, it was issued less than 15 years ago, you were at least 16 when it was issued, and it is under your name (if you have changed your name, such as by getting married, you must be able to document the name change).

After requesting a renewal, it may take up to six weeks to receive your renewed passport. If you request expedited service, it may take up to three weeks.

As a U.S. citizen, you can also easily correct or change information on your passport or report it lost or stolen.

What You'll Need

To apply to renew your U.S. passport, you'll need to fill out the form DS-82: U.S. Passport Renewal Application for Eligible Individuals and submit it along with the necessary accompanying documents. You'll need to include your current passport, two color biometric passport photos, and the applicable fee. If you have changed your name since your current passport was issued, you must submit your marriage certificate or court order documenting the change (originals only, no copies).

Fees

The fee differs depending on the type of passport you are applying for. If you would like the classic book-type passport, you'll have to pay $110. If you're applying for a passport card, the fee is $30. To obtain both, you must combine the fees and pay $140.

Regardless of the type of passport you're applying for, you must submit the same form.

Locations

To apply for your passport renewal, you must visit a USPS office or other qualifying location in Puerto Rico. To find passport locations near you, simply search your ZIP code or city in the passport location finder.

If you are not applying in person, you must send your passport application to the address designated for your state. Applicants in Puerto Rico should send their applications to the following address:

National Passport Processing Center
P.O. Box 90155
Philadelphia, PA 19190-0155

If you are applying for passport renewal from outside the United States or Canada, visit your nearest U.S. embassy or consulate for information on application procedures.

Passport Offices

Passport offices all over Puerto Rico can handle passport and passport renewal requests from U.S. citizens residing in Puerto Rico. Appointments are mandatory for application renewals. Here are some of the biggest passport offices in Puerto Rico:

Plaza Las Americas Office – San Juan
Franklyn D. Roosevelt Ave.
3rd Floor Local 615,
Plaza Las Américas
San Juan, Puerto Rico 00919
Hours of service: 8:00 a.m. to 4:00 p.m., Monday to Saturday

Passport Office – Ponce
Ponce Services Building
#72 Mayor St., Suite 180
Ponce, Puerto Rico 00730
Hours of service: 8:00 a.m. to 3:00 p.m., Monday to Friday

Passport Office – Fajardo
Dr. López St. Corner Muñoz Rivera
Fajardo, Puerto Rico 00738
(Second floor of the Municipal Electronic Library)
Hours of service: 8:00 a.m. to 3:00 p.m., Monday to Friday

Passport Office – Arecibo
Arecibo City Hall, first floor
José de Diego Avenue #100
Arecibo, Puerto Rico 00612
Hours of service: 8:00 a.m. to 3:00 p.m., Monday to Friday

CSI – Mayagüez Mall
Mayagüez Mall
975 Eugenio María de Hostos Ave.
Mayagüez, Puerto Rico 00680
Hours of service: 8:00 a.m. to 4:00 p.m., Monday to Friday

Real Estate in Puerto Rico

A Caribbean dream home on a white sandy beach is one of the many draws enticing foreigners and mainland Americans to Puerto Rico. However, as in any housing market, there are certain quirks in the Puerto Rico market that can lead first-time buyers to make common mistakes. Buyers and flippers alike should educate themselves and carefully prepare in order to achieve their Caribbean dream with as few headaches as possible.

General Rules for Buying Real Estate in Puerto Rico

Weather Worries

Weather in the Caribbean can be very damaging to homes. Hurricanes can be devastating, of course, but more ordinary weather can wreak havoc too. Make sure your house or property can withstand a flood. If your home is on or near the beach, you may have to pay for additional insurance, as it will most likely be in a flood zone. Salty air from the ocean will rust stainless steel and increase maintenance for waterfront homes or those otherwise near the ocean.

Look up costs for hazard insurance on your specific property or location. Make sure your building is hurricane-proof and that your condo or property has a backup generator. If you are building or renovating, always use the most durable materials.

In addition to dangerous storms, Puerto Rico maintains hot Caribbean temperatures. Puerto Rico generally stays in the range of 80–85 degrees Fahrenheit. However, that can be very hot if your property has no wind and no pool. You will certainly need a dehumidifier for your home in Puerto Rico because of the high humidity levels. So, before you buy your home, find out the direction of the wind at each property you look at and choose the one with the best ocean breezes.

Never Buy From Photos

View the property in person before you buy. Never buy property based solely on photos online. Sometimes real estate websites or property owners simply post photos of the nearest beach, not the view you actually have. They may even share a rendering of what a dream house on the property could look like, not what it actually looks like. It is essential to view any property for yourself prior to making an offer and to understand exactly what amenities and utilities are already available at the site.

Property Inspection and History

Before making an offer, ensure your chosen property is free from any encumbrances, such as debts, liens, easements, or undisclosed owners. A licensed realtor can provide you with the property title before signing.

You can also request a more comprehensive property background check, which could encompass a professional appraisal, title search, property survey, and explanation of homeowner's association (HOA) dues. Taking these steps is strongly advised to guarantee you get exactly what you are paying for in Puerto Rico.

Inspection and Equipment

Hiring a professional property inspector in Puerto Rico is essential and costs as little as $300. A property inspector can inspect and uncover huge and costly flaws that might otherwise be overlooked.

Be sure to also inspect the equipment on the property that you wish to keep, such as any hot tub, pool engine, stove, washer/dryer, hot water heater, refrigerator, or even certain furniture. Make sure such items are included in the sales contract.

Flipping Houses in Puerto Rico

Don't Skimp on Labor

Hiring the cheapest labor available may actually prove more costly in the long run, as inexperienced laborers take longer than vetted tradespeople to do the same amount of work. And often, their work will need to be redone, as it may not be up to an owner's standards or the government's building codes. Hiring experienced tradespeople may cost more up front, but you can rest assured that their work will be done right the first time.

Expect the Unexpected

You never know what you may find after you have bought a house, even one that fully passes inspection. Unforeseen termites, hidden rot, and other shocks that balloon costs and derail schedules are not uncommon in Puerto Rico. Add a generous cushion to both your renovation timeline and budget, allowing for flexibility to your plans.

Selling Takes Time

Depending on your market, reselling your flipped property can take time and effort in Puerto Rico. When searching for property to flip, aim for waterfront homes, tourist areas, and relatively high-income neighborhoods.

Vacation or Rental Property in Puerto Rico

No Loans for Fixer-Uppers?

If you intend to buy a fixer-upper as a second home or for rental income, you may have a hard time finding loans. This is because Puerto Rican lenders, using a Federal Housing Administration (FHA) 203k loan, will only finance both purchase and repairs for *primary* residences, not secondary residences. Secondary homes will only be financed if all necessary repairs are completed. Thus, buying an FHA "as is" foreclosed home may be relatively cheap, but if you have to spend all your personal savings to purchase it, with no money for repairs, you may be putting yourself at great financial risk.

Condo Fees and HOA Rules

If you intend to rent out your condo, make sure the condo's HOA rules allow for short-term rentals. Many do not. If you have pets, verify whether or not your condo allows them. Condo fees themselves are worth investigating, too—do they include insurance, pool or gym keys, utilities, etc.? Even parking spaces are worth a closer inspection. Ask about how many are included with your deed and the cost to rent additional spaces, if needed.

Home Loans in Puerto Rico

Puerto Rico is a United States territory. All laws, including those governing loans, must follow U.S. federal regulations in addition to those on the island. As such, the process of applying for a loan in Puerto Rico is often very similar to that of the mainland United States.

As in the rest of the United States, your credit report will be run by the lender. Be sure to check your credit score yourself before seeking a pre-approval for a home loan to avoid any potential setbacks or delays.

Documents to Provide

- Two years of W-2s and tax returns
- A recent 30 days' worth of paystubs
- Bank statements for two months
- Quote for homeowner's insurance

- All financial information regarding any homes or businesses you own
- Paper trails for any recent withdrawals or deposits over $1000
- Your business's financial statements from the previous year if you are self-employed

Tips for First-Time Home Buyers

There are more costs to buying a home than the price of the property. Realtor fees, insurance fees, closing costs, and repairs can sap your savings and put first-time buyers in an unexpected bind. Such payments and up-front costs can be prohibitive and ruinous if buyers are weighed down by a mass of other payments already, such as a child's tuition, car payments, loan payments, etc., not to mention the costs of utilities and maintenance of the home. It is better to choose a smaller home that requires less upfront costs and less upkeep than a "dream" home that will drown a buyer in debt.

Never pay out of pocket for a home if it means depleting your savings. You at least need an emergency fund to fall back on. Speak to several different lenders about what they are able to offer. One may try to force you into high monthly payments or interest rates, while another could save you thousands with a simple reduction in penalties. Know your options and never risk your savings.

A Guide to Getting a Mortgage in Puerto Rico

A dream home on the "Island of Enchantment" is an enticing proposition to many homebuyers. But potential buyers should be advised that there are many special considerations when looking for a mortgage in Puerto Rico.

As in the mainland United States, in order to get the best interest rate on your mortgage in Puerto Rico, it is important to maintain a credit score as high as possible, with a debt-to-income ratio as low as possible.

The Mortgage Process

1. **Credit Reports**

   Request credit reports from the three federal credit reporting agencies: Experian, Equifax, and TransUnion. Do this at least two months before applying for a loan. Carefully review them for any mistakes or omissions and request corrections, if necessary.

2. **Loan Officer**

   Your loan officer can issue a pre-qualification, a document that indicates what types of loans you qualify for, the amount the bank will lend you, and your monthly payment. This can save much time down the road when you are looking for a home. Visit your loan officer, and be sure to bring the following documentation:

- Copies of your tax information for the last two years
- Proof of employment and recent payroll
- Bank statements or evidence of funds for closing fees and down payment
- Creditor and debt information
- Retirement plan information

3. **Home Search and Loan Application**

Hire a local real estate agent in Puerto Rico, as not all listings are found online. Look for homes in your desired areas. Once you have made a decision, apply for a mortgage through one of the options listed.

4. **Loan Processing**

A mortgage analyst will verify your income, debts, and assets to determine which mortgage product best fits your needs. They will also appraise the value of the property and determine what funds are available to close the loan.

5. **Closing**

The buyer and seller will sign the deed to the property before a notary, who will then inscribe the transaction in the property registry. The buyer usually pays for the appraisal, plot plan, title study, certified deed stamps and vouchers, flood certification, credit report, and various policies. The seller typically pays for the sales agreement fees, deed cancellation fees, real estate agent's commission, and the original sales agreement deed stamps. With the mortgage process complete, you will now be the owner of your own Puerto Rico home.

Types of Mortgages Available in Puerto Rico

Fixed-Rate or Adjustable-Rate?

A fixed-rate mortgage means the interest rate stays fixed at a percentage for the entire duration of the loan. The interest rate stays the same, meaning the monthly payment stays the same.

An adjustable-rate mortgage (ARM) means the interest rate changes on a set frequency (e.g., every year). Hybrid ARMs are ARMS that begin as fixed-rate loans for several years and then transition to ARMs for the remainder of the loan. With either of these types of loans, the interest rate can go up over time and stretch a borrower's budget beyond its limit.

FHA Loans

FHA loans are backed by the Federal Housing Administration's mortgage insurance program. FHA loans in Puerto Rico are open to anyone, not just first-time homebuyers. Down payments with FHA loans can be as low as 3.5%, which means greatly decreased costs at closing.

With an FHA loan, down payment and closing costs can be paid in several ways:

- By a government agency or charitable organization to help low- and moderate-income families or first-time homebuyers
- By a relative
- By an employer or labor union
- By a friend with a documented interest in the borrower

Bear in mind that FHA loans are only available for existing homes intended for primary use. If you are looking to Puerto Rico for a second home, for vacation rental property, or to build a new house, FHA loans will not apply. Also, borrowers will need to factor the cost of mortgage insurance into their monthly payments.

Conforming/Conventional Loans

Conforming loans, also known as conventional mortgages, are mortgages that adhere to the guidelines and loan limits of the Federal National Mortgage Association (Fannie Mae) and the Federal Home Loan Mortgage Corporation (Freddie Mac). Fannie Mae/Freddie Mac mortgages typically require a minimum down payment of 5%, though two mortgages available through Fannie Mae only require a 3% down payment.

Though sometimes more costly, Fannie Mae and Freddie Mac loans are the most popular options for second-home purchases in Puerto Rico.

Other Mortgage Options

"Non-conforming loans" are mortgages that do not conform to the lending guidelines of government-backed loans such as FHA or Freddie Mac. This could be due to property condition, credit issues, or intended usage of the property (commercial, investment, etc.). As interest rates and closing costs are higher with non-conforming loans, they are more expensive than conforming options.

"Cooperatives" are privately owned Puerto Rican lending banks under the supervision of the Public Corporation for the Supervision and Insurance of Cooperatives in Puerto Rico (COSSEC). When in the market for land, wooden homes, or mixed-material construction, it is highly advisable to seek a loan from a local cooperative.

To qualify for a cooperative's loan products, prospective buyers must first purchase stock in the cooperative. The advantage of cooperatives is that they are more flexible in the ways they grant loan approval and offer extraordinarily convenient options for both land and construction financing. The Cooperativa de Credito de Ahorro de Isabela and the Cooperativa de Rincón are both highly recommended in Puerto Rico.

Types of Lenders in Puerto Rico

Primary Lenders

These lenders can originate, process, approve, and close their own loans. Examples in Puerto Rico include Banco Popular de Puerto Rico, First Mortgage, and Scotiabank. These lenders have many locations throughout Puerto Rico and offer a wide array of mortgage products, making them very convenient. They are also quite technologically savvy compared to less corporatized lenders on the island.

Secondary Lenders

These lenders do not have the ability to approve mortgage loans, though they are able to originate, process, and close mortgage loans. These lenders depend on primary lenders for approval and funding and thus are slower to process. Primary lenders may impose stricter loan criteria on borrowers if made through a secondary lender. Local Puerto Rico examples of secondary lenders include RF Mortgage and SunWest.

Buying HUD Homes in Puerto Rico

Some houses in Puerto Rico are owned by the United States Department of Housing and Urban Development (HUD), typically due to foreclosure. You must not have bought another HUD home within two years prior to your offer and must agree to occupy the home for at least one year. HUD does not directly offer mortgages on foreclosed HUD homes, but buyers can obtain financing through a traditional source, such as a lender or bank.

The Bidding Process

To buy a house owned by HUD, buyers must place an online bid on the property through an agent or broker who is registered with HUD. Buyers must provide their agent with a pre-qualification letter from a loan officer or lender confirming their ability to finance the home before submitting an online offer for said home.

Depending on the asking price of the HUD home, buyers are required to submit a deposit of between $500 and $1,000 with their online bid. This deposit is returned if a bid is declined. If a buyer's bid is approved, they will only have 24 hours to sign all forms, including the initial sales agreement.

Closing on a HUD property usually takes place between 30 and 60 days after the initial signing. HUD's own purchasing contracts, deadlines, and requirements must be met to close on the property. HUD will even pay your broker's commission, provided it is included in the contract.

"As Is" Properties

Bidding online for a foreclosed home can be a great way to save money when moving to Puerto Rico. However, there is a catch: HUD homes are sold "as is," with no warranty, meaning HUD will neither pay nor correct any defects or damages on the property whatsoever. The new owner is required to make all repairs, and while repairs may be quite simple, an "as is" home could also require extensive, and expensive, renovation.

Be sure to pay for a professional home inspection before submitting your online bid to buy a HUD home in Puerto Rico or elsewhere. It may save you a lot of money and spare you a lot of headaches.

Anticipating Potential Issues

Language Barrier

English is the official language of Puerto Rico, as it is a U.S. territory. However, not everyone on the island is fluent in English. It is strongly advisable not to enter into the mortgage process unless you are fluent in Spanish or have a Spanish-speaking lawyer or other aide in your corner.

Locking in a Rate

Expect some difficulty with locking in a mortgage rate from a bank in Puerto Rico. Your 5% rate may be for the duration of the loan or unexpectedly rise to 5.5% a few months later. It may not be quite clear what you are getting.

Disorganized Closing

Title-keeping and property records in Puerto Rico can be somewhat lax and disorganized compared to the mainland United States. Though not always, it is possible you may find some documents to be incomplete, and others may be missing. It is essential to work with a local expert in Puerto Rican real estate law and mortgages to avoid potential headaches during the closing process.

Refinancing Your Mortgage in Puerto Rico

In Puerto Rico, refinancing a mortgage means applying for a new mortgage. Once it is approved, you must pay new closing costs and/or additional fees. Consider whether paying these additional costs is worth the refinanced rate.

Where to Live on the Island

There are many unique regions in Puerto Rico, each with its own amenities and features. With an array of locations to choose from, there is a high likelihood of finding your ideal neighborhood. With our guide, you will have no trouble finding what area is best suited for you.[3]

<u>We have looked into nine popular living spots:</u>

1. Old San Juan (San Juan)
2. Condado (San Juan)
3. Miramar (San Juan)
4. Isla Verde (San Juan)
5. Guaynabo and Bayamon (San Juan)
6. Dorado
7. Bahia
8. Palmas del Mar
9. Rincon

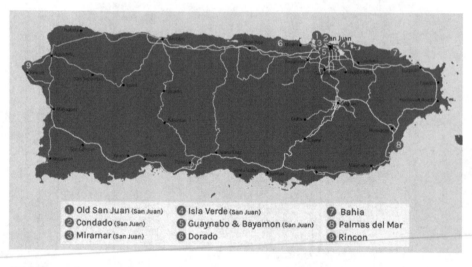

1. Old San Juan (San Juan) 4. Isla Verde (San Juan) 7. Bahia
2. Condado (San Juan) 5. Guaynabo & Bayamon (San Juan) 8. Palmas del Mar
3. Miramar (San Juan) 6. Dorado 9. Rincon

Old San Juan

Safety: Good
Cost profile: High
Walkability: High
Population density: High
Travel time to SJU airport: 15 minutes

---

[3] All area home prices are as of November 2021

Founded over 500 years ago, the island of Old San Juan is widely known and visited for its historical significance. Popular with residents and locals alike, the area is teeming with life and color, from assorted boutique shops and busy restaurants, to beautiful Spanish architecture and more.

The cobblestone streets are ideal for exploring on foot, bike, or the free trolley system. History lovers can indulge in hundreds of 16th and 17th century buildings that have been restored and are open to the public, including the three forts of Old San Juan—El Morro, San Cristóbal, and San Gerónimo.

Due to the wide variety of people living here, home buyers with different budgets have several purchasing options available to them. Most of the residential housing consists of three- to four-story row homes and multi-family structures. Prices change significantly depending on the size, unit, and location within this area. You can find units ranging from 300 square feet to more than 5,000 square feet, and prices from $230,000 to over $2.5 million. Rent in Old San Juan is reasonable, with a 900-square-foot property in a good area coming in at $1,500 per month.

Condado

Safety: Good
Cost profile: High
Walkability: High
Population density: High
Travel time to SJU airport: 10 minutes

Just a few minutes from Old San Juan, Condado sits on a beautiful beach strip. The pedestrian focused region is a popular residential spot known for its peace and tranquility, as well as having a good police presence and a feeling of security. An array of different restaurants, shops, and casinos serve as fun destinations with the beach only a few steps away. Condado is known for having one of the most beautiful beach areas—Ocean Park. Outdoor activities are big in the area, including paddle boarding, surfing, kitesurfing, volleyball, beach tennis, and more.

Living spaces in the region offer a good mix of condos and houses, averaging $650,000 for a multi-room condo. Prices start in the mid $200,000s for a nice, quaint apartment, and go as high as $8 million for a penthouse beachfront unit atop a high rise condominium. A 900-square-foot rental can be found for as low as $1,600 per month.

Miramar

Safety: Average
Cost profile: Average
Walkability: Average
Population density: High
Travel time to SJU airport: 10 minutes

Serving as one of the two entrances to Old San Juan, the historic district of Miramar is a great location for anyone looking to be close enough to the action while enjoying more space and quiet. The more residential community appeals to families with children and retirees coming from the mainland United States.

The neighborhood is home to the recently constructed Puerto Rico Convention Center that connects to the sweeping green lawns and gently spraying fountains of the Paseo de las Fuentes park. Many restaurants are also located in the area, providing several dining options. The Club Nautico de San Juan offers sailing enthusiasts access to a boating club, sailing lessons, and fishing events. The club hosts the annual International Billfish Tournament that lures in fishermen from around the world.

Miramar offers a more elegant neighborhood, with townhouse/condo-style housing and Spanish-style houses replete with patios and gardens. Even with a few trophy properties exceeding a $2 million price tag, housing costs in Miramar are lower than in Old San Juan or Condado, but have increased significantly in the past two years. Prices for condos come in under $400,000, while houses generally start in the $600,000 range. Rent in the area has increased, with a 900-square-foot property as low as $1,500 per month.

Isla Verde

Safety: Average
Cost profile: Average
Walkability: Average
Population density: High
Travel time to SJU airport: 5 minutes

Directly north of SJU airport is the popular social spot of Isla Verde. The busy area is home to many activities, most of them found in hotels and high rises. Apart from residential condominiums, the area hosts countless hotels that offer visitors direct access to the beaches. The coast is lined with restaurants and lounges, some of them even offering dining tables and projected movies on the sand. Rooftop lounges, nightclubs, and casinos offer great nightlife activities. The island's largest casino is Caguas, and is part of the Four Points by Sheraton Caguas Real Hotel & Casino.

Searching for real estate in Isla Verde is rewarding considering that, compared to other popular destinations, it has more units on the market at any given time. With a good mix of condos and residential homes with close proximity to San Juan, finding a spot for $300,000 is common. Luxurious properties in the area can exceed the $1 million price tag, though most homes cost less than $800,000. Rent in Isla Verde is relatively inexpensive with, 900-square-foot apartments available for as low as $1,300 per month.

Guaynabo and Bayamon

Safety: Average
Cost profile: Low
Walkability: Low
Population density: High
Travel time to SJU airport: 30 minutes

Sitting four miles apart from each other, Guaynabo and Bayamon are considered one by many. Home to about 250,000 residents, this region is detached from the busy San Juan city and beach commotion. Offering a much more residential feel, this region is home to several industries covering healthcare, social aid, finance, insurance, retail trade, educational services, tech, and more. About 20 minutes inland, Guaynabo and Bayamon have several restaurants and popular attractions. You can find one of the island's most beautiful waterfalls, Poza Prieta Waterfall, hidden in Bayamon, along a 42-acre science museum. For great authentic Puerto Rican food, Guaynabo has many places offering delicious and inexpensive bites.

Only a few miles from the capital, real estate prices significantly drop. It is possible to find a nice property with a yard for under $250,000. Investing $400,000 for a new residence in the area will get you far. Residences of all sizes are available. Large properties can be found for $5,000 per month, but overall, rent is low, with large 3-bedroom apartments costing $1,800 per month.

Dorado

Safety: Good
Cost profile: High
Walkability: Low
Population density: Low
Travel time to SJU airport: 35 minutes

About 30 minutes west of San Juan, Dorado offers residents ocean views from quiet and peaceful neighborhoods. A hot place for tourists, surfers, and boaters, the hotels, golf courses, tennis courts, and beaches draw in visitors looking for a break from the action in San Juan. With about 40,000 residents, 10% of San Juan's population, getting in and out of Dorado is rarely a problem. While Dorado is amenity rich, the commute and traffic to and from San Juan for business and pleasure should be a consideration. Oftentimes, transportation like Uber is only available from San Juan, not to it. On the plus side, Dorado is close to all cities and locales toward the western part of the island.

Real estate prices in the Dorado Beach Resort are some of the highest on the island, almost always exceeding $2 million. If you choose to live outside of the gated portion, prices revert back to around $250,000 for a 3-bedroom, 3-bath property.

Bahia

Safety: Good
Cost profile: High
Walkability: Low
Population density: Low
Travel time to SJU airport: 35 minutes

Located in the northeast of the Island, Bahia is blooming with nature and tranquility. Bahia Beach Resort is affiliated with the St. Regis, a popular alternative to Dorado's Ritz Carlton.

Similar to Dorado, if you decide to live here, you'll be more isolated from the metro area and with less population. Living near Rio Grande, the closest city to Bahia, does enable quicker access to the coastal city of Fajardo, the most popular place to store a boat with quick access to the islands of Culebra and Vieques. You will also be closer to El Yunque, the sprawling rainforest national park.

Real estate here is generally cheaper than Dorado, but with less options. The starting purchase price for living inside one of the golf course communities is $250,000.

Palmas del Mar

Safety: Good
Cost profile: Average
Walkability: Average
Population density: Average
Travel time to SJU airport: 1 Hour

Residents of Palmas del Mar, near the city of Humacao, love to tout the strong sense of community and family. Located in the southeast corner of Puerto

Rico, one hour from San Juan, this is a popular location to live "away from San Juan." Living here is affordable, amenity-rich, and nearly on the beach. Similar to the city of Fajardo just to the north, Palmas is a boating mecca with some of the best boating infrastructure. One thing to consider is your travel time to San Juan, and how your social and entertainment options may be reduced by living outside of the main city.

Real estate here is varied, with many price points and developments from which to choose. Starting at $400,000 you can live within a community on the beach.

Rincon

Safety: Good
Cost profile: Low
Walkability: Average
Population density: Low
Travel time to SJU airport: 2.5 hours

Quiet and peaceful, Rincon is nestled in the westernmost end of the island, about two hours from San Juan. With open views of the Atlantic, the smaller beaches have not yet been taken over by hotels. You'll find a very "local" feel here, albeit with many expats who relish the outdoors. Rincon is famous for surfing, which draws in people from around the world, especially during surf competitions. Despite being far from San Juan, Rincon has the infrastructure and services to support your needs, and the needs of families and business owners alike. The major city of Mayaguez is just to the south, and offers a small airport and common shops.

Real estate here is generally very affordable, with small houses starting at $150,000. If you like the vibes of Rincon, you should also take a look at the nearby coastal cities of Aguadilla and Isabela.

	Safety	Cost Profile	Walkability	Population Density	Travel Time to SJU Airport
Old San Juan	Good	High	High	High	15 minutes
Condado	Good	High	High	High	10 minutes
Miramar	Average	Average	Average	High	10 minutes
Isla Verde	Average	Average	Average	High	5 minutes
Guaynabo & Bayamon	Average	Low	Low	High	30 minutes
Dorado	Good	High	Low	Low	35 minutes
Bahia	Good	High	Low	Low	35 minutes
Palmas del Mar	Good	Average	Average	Average	1 hour
Rincon	Good	Low	Average	Low	2.5 hours

Getting a Puerto Rican Driver's License

Puerto Rico may be part of the United States, but that does not mean that your U.S. state driver's license is valid in the small island territory. Within 30 days of moving to Puerto Rico, new residents must apply for a local driver's license. If you have come to Puerto Rico to take advantage of its many tax incentives, you have to obtain a Puerto Rican driver's license immediately after purchasing a property or signing a lease contract. The default procedure to apply for a Puerto Rico driver's license involves receiving a Learner's Permit Certificate and waiting at least 30 days before obtaining the full Puerto Rico license, but the process is a bit faster for those who already hold a valid U.S. license.

Reciprocity Categories

In the past, Puerto Rico had differing levels of reciprocity with different states, with a lucky few enjoying full reciprocity, an unlucky few subject to no reciprocity, and most in the category of partial reciprocity. However, as of 2014, all states have full reciprocity agreements in place.

This means that people with a valid U.S. driver's license do not have to take the written or driving tests to obtain a Puerto Rican driver's license. However, as the result of a change in regulations, they are now required to attend an hour-long drug and alcohol course. These classes are offered at all CESCO (the DMV of Puerto Rico) offices across the island, but applicants must confirm available dates and times directly with their specific CESCO office. We recommend scheduling an appointment with CESCO. CESCO's offices can be found in Aguadilla, Arecibo, Bayamón, Caguas, Fajardo, Guayama, Humacao, Manatí, Mayagüez, Río Piedras, Ponce, Barranquitas, and Utuado.

In contrast to applicants with a valid U.S. driver's license, if an applicant's license is expired, they must take both the written and driving test, but they do not have to wait 30 days.

Applicants are required to surrender their current state license so that they do not hold two licenses. It is advised to obtain another state-issued identification card to ease procedures with ID checkers in the United States, as not all realize that Puerto Rico is part of the United States.

Necessary Documents

There are several documents applicants need to bring to the CESCO office to obtain a driver's license:

- Your current U.S. driver's license
- An official copy of your state driving record

- A document that shows your Social Security number (bringing your official Social Security card is recommended; bear in mind that it cannot be laminated)
- Your birth certificate or U.S. passport
- Two forms of proof of residence (e.g., utility bill or bank statement in your name and less than 60 days old)
- A filled-out DTOP-DIS-257 form
- Stamps (purchasable at a CESCO office or bank)
    - Hacienda stamps (code 5120): $16
    - Comprobante REAL ID proof stamps (code 0842): $2
    - Comprobante proof stamps (code 2028): $17
    - Comprobante proof stamps (code 0842): $2
- Medical statement (DTOP-DIS-260) ($20–$25)

Most states will send you an official copy of your driving record for less than $10, and some states even allow you to download an official copy from the internet. Make sure you know which category your state falls under, as the CESCO will reject the document if you download and print a nonofficial copy.

For the Hacienda stamps, make sure to purchase them at the bank or CESCO office, where you will pay the true value. You can also find second-hand sellers near the DMV, but they add a premium, so you will end up paying more than you need to.

Regarding the medical statement, all you need is a doctor to officially state that you're healthy enough to drive. You can find numerous doctor's offices around the CESCO, and the procedure consists merely of answering a few health-related questions and having the doctor fill out a form and sign it. Some CESCO offices, such as the one in Bayamon, even feature on-site doctors from whom you can obtain the certification.

Hire an expediter

This is optional, but it can dramatically speed up and smooth out the process. An expediter will guide you through the entire process, making sure you have the correct documentation, arranging for all the necessary paperwork to be completed, scheduling your courses (if necessary), and navigating you through the CESCO building. Given that dealings with the DMV and similar institutions are generally a headache, even if you could complete the process on your own, many believe the peace of mind is worth the extra fee. This is especially useful if you don't speak Spanish well. One such expediter is License & Co., who charges $130.00 for the reciprocity process.

Confirm the information

Before you leave the CESCO, double-check the expiry date and information printed on your newly issued license. Unlike the DMV in the United States, the CESCO does not ask you to verify the information before they print it on the license, which could lead to mistakes in your address or name. You will need to get the license reprinted if you find mistakes, and it's best to do so as soon as you can.

REAL ID

It is not mandatory to make your driver's license into a REAL ID, but it is highly recommended. Starting on May 3, 2023, you will need either your passport or your REAL ID to take domestic flights or enter federal facilities. The procedure is the same—with the addition of the DTOP-DIS-328 form—and the REAL ID looks almost identical to the default driver's license, except that it contains a star in the right corner. Make sure to bring the extra money for the REAL ID.

To receive your REAL ID, you must be present during the process at all times. You can receive REAL ID licenses at the CESCOs in Carolina, Bayamon, Arecibo, Aguadilla, Ponce, Guayama, and Humacao.

Translated English Forms

Bureaucracy is a nuisance even in your native language—in a foreign language, it's a nightmare. To facilitate the process of applying for a Puerto Rican driver's license, we have translated the forms DTOP-DIS-257 (driver's license application), DTOP-DIS-260 (medical statement for a driver's license application), and DTOP-DIS-328 (REAL ID application) into English.

The easy-to-understand forms are in PDF format, with checkboxes or blanks waiting for your input. When you enter your answers into the form, they will automatically show up on the Spanish form, leaving you with a perfectly completed Spanish form you can print out and present to CESCO.

Buying a Car

Buying and Servicing a Car in Puerto Rico

Buying a car on the island isn't a necessity, of course—some may have their car shipped from the mainland. However, the process is complicated and expensive. Others may choose to forgo a car altogether, but even in this case, obtaining a Puerto Rican driver's license is recommended as a contribution to the "closer connection" bona fide residency test.

Where to Buy a Car in Puerto Rico

Prospective car buyers rejoice: car dealerships are abundant across Puerto Rico. Toyota, Hyundai, Honda, and Lincoln are popular brands, each with a number of dealerships spanning the island, so no matter where you live in Puerto Rico, you can likely find one of these dealerships near you. If you're in the market for a luxury car, you can also stop by the Lamborghini, Jaguar, Porsche or BMW dealerships in San Juan. Volkswagen, Chrysler, Mazda, Kia, and other makers also have a presence in Puerto Rico, allowing most car buyers ample resources to find the right car for them.

Of course, the number of car dealerships on the island is too high for us to list them all in this article. If you'd like the address, website, and phone number of Puerto Rican car dealerships, reach out to us at info@relocatepuertorico.com for an Excel spreadsheet of the top dealerships on the island.

The Process to Purchase a Used Car

If you would prefer to buy a used car from a private owner, this section details the procedures to follow.

Craft a Bill of Sale

Once you find a car that you like from a private seller and strike up an oral agreement to purchase the car, you need to move the agreement to paper to legalize it. For this, you need to craft a bill of sale. The exact form can differ, but it must be a legally binding agreement that stipulates all necessary conditions of the transaction.

We at PRelocate have a template for a bill of sale, and we would be happy to provide it to any of our clients who request it. Please reach out to us at info@relocatepuertorico.com for more information.

Make the Payment

How much you will pay is decided in negotiations between you and the seller, but you must pay the amount that both parties agree upon and write down on the bill of sale. Assuming you do not need to take out a loan to purchase the car, you can make the payment in cash, through a manager's check, or via a wire transfer. You must determine the payment method with the seller, but bear in mind that wire transfers, for example, incur a fee.

Go to a Notary

For the transaction to be legally recognized, both the buyer and seller must go to a notary for the title. Both parties must be physically present, and the document must be filled out correctly. It is entirely in Spanish, so if your Spanish is not quite up to speed, familiarizing yourself with the content of the document in advance may be a wise idea. Bringing along a trusted Spanish speaker may also bring you peace of mind.

Buy Stamps

For the transfer of the title, you will require "sellos," which are government stamps used instead of money to pay for government processes. You can purchase sellos at a bank, but there are also various stores and locations that offer both sellos and notary services. If you would like to look into these alternative locations, simply let us know.

Transfer the Title

Once you have completed all the above steps, you are ready to initiate the official process of transferring the title. After transferring the money to the seller, visit your local DTOP office with your signed and notarized title, the executed bill of sale, and your government stamps and have the officials process the title transfer. They will provide you with a title in your name and the respective license. Then, the car is officially and legally yours. Enjoy your newfound mobility across the island of Puerto Rico.

Where to Have a Car Serviced in Puerto Rico

Once you've found the right car, you'll need to take care of it, and that involves getting it serviced every now and then. In fact, you may need to have your car serviced more often in Puerto Rico than what you're used to in the mainland United States—the natural result of the poor road conditions of certain areas combined with the more outgoing driving behavior found across the island. On the upside, though, in sunny Puerto Rico, you don't have to change over to winter tires every year.

Mechanics populate all areas of the island, making it fairly easy to locate one. However, the easiest place to get new tires and car service is often Costco. Costco lets you buy tires as well as schedule them for installation at their premises, streamlining the process of obtaining new tires.
If you'd prefer to have your car serviced at a traditional mechanic instead, Puerto Rico offers plenty of choices.

Vehicle Registration

If you want to drive a car in Puerto Rico, you will need a car tag, or "marbete" in Spanish, which is issued by the Department of Transportation and Public Works (DTOP by its Spanish acronym) or authorized inspection centers. All authorized inspection centers must display a sign stating they are "DTOP-authorized." Your marbete will have one month punched, and you will be required to renew it each year on that month. The government does not usually send out renewal reminders, so it's up to you to remember, and failure to renew your marbete can result in hefty fines or having your car towed, so make sure you don't forget.

How to Renew Your Marbete

There are four main things you need to renew your marbete: vehicle registration, inspection, insurance, and the marbete fee.

Vehicle Registration

In order to obtain or renew your marbete, you need to renew your vehicle registration. The government should mail the registration form to you 30 to 40 days prior to the renewal date, but you can also print off the form from the DTOP website. You can print the form off whenever you wish, but you can only use the registration to renew your marbete within 45 days of expiry or if the marbete has already expired.

Vehicle Inspection

The next step to obtaining or renewing your marbete is having your car inspected. This is like an annual health checkup but for cars—the purpose is to identify any mechanical issues that could pose safety hazards for you or others. Cars are not required to be inspected until they are at least two years old, so if you have a brand-new car, you can skip the inspection this time. You must present your vehicle registration in paper when you have your car inspected, and you must have it inspected in the same month you obtain the marbete.

Insurance

Every vehicle in Puerto Rico is required to be insured, whether privately or through "compulsory insurance." If you have private car insurance, you need to request a certificate of insurance from your insurance company. If you do not have and cannot get private insurance, you will be required to purchase Puerto Rico's compulsory insurance.

When you obtain or renew your marbete at an authorized entity (including official inspection stations, banks, or Coperativa [bank and trust]), simply include the insurance fee along with your registration fee and request compulsory insurance, which will be granted for one year. You will be given a selection form and may choose the insurer you wish to be insured by.

Get Your Marbete

Once you have your vehicle registration, inspection, and insurance (or money for the compulsory insurance), simply go to an authorized entity and present the above documentation along with an $85 fee for the marbete. Once the payment is processed, you will receive your stamp registration and receipt along with your new marbete.

Finally, the last step is to physically replace the marbete. Make sure to replace the marbete only after the month for which it is punched has begun, as you aren't allowed to use marbete tags with future dates.

Setting Up Electricity, Water, and Internet

Electricity, water, and the Internet are three things we can't live without, so you'll want to get these set up as soon as you move to Puerto Rico so you can settle into your new home as quickly as possible. As with most bureaucratic processes, setting up these essentials will require time and lots of personal information and identification documents, but ultimately, it isn't that hard.

How to Set Up Electricity

In order to set up electricity at your new home, you need to visit the Puerto Rico Electric Power Authority (PREPA) office in person and present all the necessary documentation for installation. Prepare to wait at least a week for the setup to be complete, as the process typically takes between five to seven business days. The information and documentation you need to provide differs depending on whether you are contracting a new electrical service or service for an existing property, as well as whether you own the property or are renting it.

New Service

To have electricity set up at a new property, you must provide the following information about yourself and your spouse, if you have one:

- Your full name
- Your marital status
- Your Social Security number
- Your driver's license or passport
- Your workplace
- Your work and residential telephone number
- The property's physical address
- Your postal address, if different from the physical address (such as a virtual mailbox)
- A picture of your meter showing the serial number
- A down payment of between $100 and $150 (PREPA will indicate the exact amount when you apply for service)
- A Certification of Electrical Installation, which is obtainable from a professional electrician with a valid license (this document is needed if the property is new or has been without service for more than a year)
- If you are the owner:

    o The purchase agreement or deed of property

- If you are renting:

- o The rental or lease agreement
- o The name, address, and phone number of the property owner

Service for an Existing Property

To set up electrical service in your name for an existing property that already has electrical service, you will need to provide the following information:

- Your full name
- Your marital status
- Your Social Security number
- Your driver's license or passport
- Your workplace
- Your work and residential telephone number
- If you are renting:

  - o The rental or lease agreement
  - o The name, address, and phone number of the property owner

New Service at a Commercial Property

If you have opened or plan to open a business with a physical location in Puerto Rico, you will also have to have electricity set up at your company's building. To set up the service, you will be required to present the following information:

- The full name of the company owner or the company name
- A Certification of Electrical Installation, which is obtainable from a professional electrician with a valid license (this document is needed if the property is new or has been without service for more than a year)
- A use permit, granted by OGPe or the corresponding autonomous municipality, if the property is new or if there is a change in its use
- A down payment (PREPA will indicate the exact amount when you apply for service)
- A picture of your meter showing the serial number
- If an individual is requesting the electrical service, they must provide the following information about themselves and their spouse, if they have one:

  - o Their full name
  - o Their marital status

122

- o Their Social Security number
- o Their driver's license or passport
- o Their workplace
- o Their work and residential telephone number

- If the business entity is a corporation:

  - o Its Certificate of Incorporation
  - o Its Certificate of Existence or Authorization to Do Business in Puerto Rico (must be less than six months old)
  - o Its Certificate of Validity or Good Standing Certificate (must be less than six months old)
  - o A memorandum from the board of directors authorizing the request of electrical service
  - o Its Employer Identification Number (EIN)

- If the business entity is a commercial or special company:

  - o A constitution deed
  - o An Agreement of Compensation and Continuous and Unlimited Guarantee (SE)
  - o The company's physical address
  - o The company's postal address, if different from the physical address

- If you own the property:

  - o The purchase agreement or deed of property

- If you are renting:

  - o The rental or lease agreement
  - o The name, address, and phone number of the property owner

Mi Cuenta Online System

On PREPA's website, you can access online services through a special portal called Mi Cuenta, as long as you are registered on PREPA's system. On the Mi Cuenta system, you can conveniently view and pay your bills online. The portal also allows users to request various services, such as electrical service for an existing property, a transfer of service, a disconnection of service, validation for electronic certificates, and tree trimming or streetlight services. Additionally, the portal provides a way for users to submit a bill objection, if necessary.

Autopayments

Autopayments are the easiest way to pay your electricity bill—that's one less thing on your plate and more time you can dedicate to growing your business. To set up autopayments with PREPA, you need to visit them in person and present your most recent PREPA bill, personal ID, payment method information, and a voided check. If the account is not in your name, you are also required to obtain an authorization letter from the account holder to make changes and updates, as well as a copy of their ID.

PREPA Website: https://aeepr.com/en-us
Email: serviciosweb@prepa.com
Phone Number: (787) 521-3434

How to Set Up Water Service

Water service in Puerto Rico is provided by Autoridad de Acueductos y Alcantarillados de Puerto Rico, or AAA. You must be prepared to wait up to two weeks for your water service to be set up: Activation can take anywhere between seven and 14 days. You can request the activation service in person or via email, but it can take up to three days to receive a response if you make a request via email.

To set up water service at your Puerto Rican home, you must provide the following information:

- Your full name
- Your Social Security number
- Your ID card or driver's license
- Your physical address
- Your postal address, if different from your physical address
- Your phone number
- A picture of your water meter showing the serial number
- Plumbers Certification issued by a plumber certified by the Colegio de Maestro Plomero of Puerto Rico (if the property is new or has been out of service for more than a year)
- A down payment (AAA will indicate the exact amount when you apply for service)
- If you own the property:

    o The purchase agreement or deed of property

- If you are renting:

    o The rental or lease agreement

Autopayments

You can easily set up autopayments of your water bill through AAA's website. All you need to do is create an account, add information related to your service with AAA, and navigate to the payment options. You will need to indicate the payment method and enter the corresponding account information.

AAA Website: https://acueductospr.com/
Email: centrotelefonico03@acueductospr.com
Phone Number: (787) 620-2482

How to Set Up Internet Service

Internet service may not be as essential as electricity and water, but life in the modern world is more or less impossible without it. Puerto Rico has a number of Internet service providers throughout the island that you can choose from to connect your home to the rest of the world. Depending on the location of your home, the company you choose, and the type of service you opt for, activation time and requirements may vary, but in general, you will be required to provide the following information:

- Your full name
- Your Social Security number
- Your physical address
- Your postal address, if different from your physical address
- Your rental contract, if applicable
- A down payment or installation fee, if applicable

Depending on where in Puerto Rico your home is, you may have more or fewer Internet service provider options. Some parts of Puerto Rico don't have access to more than one Internet service provider. However, if you're moving to San Juan, Dorado, Bayamón, or another well-connected area popular among Act 20/22 (now Act 60) decree holders, you should have quite a few options to choose from.

Here are a few of the top Internet service providers in San Juan, all of which offer both residential and business Internet service:

Liberty

Liberty is a cable Internet service provider available in most areas of Puerto Rico, including San Juan, Dorado, and Bayamón. The website is accessible in English—you can change the language in the top left-hand corner—so it's easy to understand what Liberty offers. Liberty offers coverage in 94% of San Juan, and its download speeds can reach 500 Mbps under its fastest option (up to 90 Mbps under its slowest option). Prices range from $58 to $171 per month, depending on your plan.

Website: http://www.libertypr.com/
Phone Number: (787) 355-6565

Claro

Claro is another popular Internet service provider that offers DSL Internet access, with maximum speeds of 50 Mbps, to 83% of San Juan and fiber Internet, with maximum speeds of 75 Mbps, to 16%. Claro Internet packages do not include data caps, and home Internet service plans do not include streaming limits, meaning Claro Internet allows for extensive usage, even if it is slower by default than some other options. Claro's website is only available in Spanish, and prices are generally not listed online, making it a bit difficult to understand what you're getting.

Website: https://www.claropr.com/personas/
Phone Number: (787) 281-2500

Optico Fiber

Optico Fiber offers, as its name suggests, fiber Internet connection to certain neighborhoods in San Juan, Bayamón, Carolina, and Guaynabo. It has a simple and transparent website in English, so you can easily understand what you're getting. It is one of the fastest options on the island, with download and upload speeds of up to 1000 Mbps under its standard option. This plan costs $70 per month and comes with a two-year contract.

Optico Fiber also offers a "basic Internet" plan with 4 Mbps down and 1 Mbps up. This no-contract plan is available for a one-time payment of $300, which you can also choose to pay in installments of $50 over six months. Before you jump on the low prices, however, keep in mind that 4 Mbps is extremely slow—you will not be able to stream videos, and any sizeable download will take a long time.

Shipping Items Efficiently

Long-distance moves are never easy—even if Puerto Rico's many tax incentives *will* make your life easier. The bureaucratic procedures you have to complete are numerous, and transporting all your possessions, whether household items, furniture, or tools, can be a hassle. However, in addition to making your new Puerto Rican abode feel more homey, moving your possessions to Puerto Rico can help you satisfy the "closer connection" bona fide resident test requirement. Here are our recommendations for transportation companies.

Shipping Household Items

United States Postal Service (USPS)

USPS is a great option if you're only planning to ship relatively small items. USPS offers services all across the United States and its territories, including Puerto Rico, at fixed rates. You can choose from various service options, including overnight express delivery, depending on how quickly you would like to receive your goods.

Mayflower

Mayflower is a top-rated international moving company that helps U.S. residents with their moves to more than 150 countries and jurisdictions around the world, including Puerto Rico. In addition to simple transportation, the company also offers full packing and unpacking services, international move consultation services, and customs clearance services.

La Rosa Del Monte

La Rosa Del Monte is a bilingual moving services company that offers full and partial moving services for both residential and commercial customers. Their offering includes door-to-door services and packing services. They specialize in the handling, packing, and transportation of artworks and antiquities, so they are an especially good option for museums, galleries, dealers, and collectors.

U-Pack

U-Pack prides itself on offering interstate moving services at a fraction of the price of typical moving companies. The company also claims to offer faster transportation than the competition. As the name suggests, the packing is left to you, but you may also purchase packing supplies and hire help to load and unload the moving truck.

Crowley

Crowley offers shipping and logistics services for businesses in various countries and jurisdictions worldwide. They offer customs clearance and inland transportation services in addition to their air and marine transportation services and services businesses in a number of industries.

Vehicle Shipping

Before deciding to ship your vehicle to Puerto Rico, it's worth looking into buying a car on the island, whether new or used. Puerto Rico levies hefty import taxes on vehicle shipments that can amount to as much as 20 to 30% of your car's mainland value, so buying a car in Puerto Rico is often the more economical solution. Puerto Rico features a variety of car dealers, however, so finding the right car should be fairly easy. Shipping a vehicle to Puerto Rico also results in a heap of paperwork, which can eat up your time, or your money if you hire someone else to do it.

The excise tax amount differs depending on the make, model, year, and condition of your car. To obtain a quote, please visit Hacienda's website portal. It's recommended to input your vehicle identification number (VIN) for the most accurate estimate.

Shipping Electric Cars

If your car is electric, however, you can forget all about the excise tax—all-electric and plug-in hybrid cars are exempt. This way, you can save the environment and money.

Once your electric car arrives in Puerto Rico, you will need to request an exemption letter from Hacienda. Typically, the request takes about 48 hours to process, and upon approval, Hacienda will issue you a "levante" (pick-up authorization). You have to move quickly to retrieve your car and park it at your home or another lot, because if you fail to pick up your car within 48 hours, you may incur demurrage fees. This process may differ depending on the transportation company you use, since some companies will assist you with the paperwork or refer you to a concierge service that will help. Consult with your transportation company about their services before shipping your car.

Once you have your car, you'll need to register and plate it with the Puerto Rico Department of Transportation and Public Works (DTOP). You will also need to obtain a marbete. Of course, you will need to have a Puerto Rico driver's license, too.

Protecting Your Home When You're Away

If you are planning to be away from Puerto Rico for an extended period, you will have to protect your home from mold. Puerto Rico's climate is generally classified as a tropical rainforest climate, giving the island the warm, sunny weather it's known for. However, this beautiful, year-round beach weather also comes with drawbacks, including a rainy season and high humidity. The high humidity is a serious issue across Puerto Rico, as it leads to mold easily growing in buildings that are not properly dehumidified.

You Need a Dehumidifier in Puerto Rico

Unlike the United States, which houses various types of climates across its large landmass, Puerto Rico is a small island and thus features predominantly only a tropical rainforest climate. This means that no matter where you choose to live in Puerto Rico, you will be faced with high humidity that can lead to serious mold problems. The solution is to run both a dehumidifier and an air purifier almost 24/7.

Dehumidifiers take excess moisture out of the air and deposit it in their accompanying water bin. It's not worth it to buy low-quality, cheap appliances that will break easily or not do the job properly, since you need these appliances to keep your home—and, by extension, you and your family—healthy. Humidity can also harm electronics, so if you plan to keep the windows of your apartment open on a regular basis, it's best to keep the dehumidifier in your office or computer room with the door shut.

The need for constant dehumidification in Puerto Rico can present problems if you are planning to be away for extended periods of time. If you leave Puerto Rico for a while and do not leave the dehumidifier running, you may be greeted by mold all over your things when you return home. Be careful, though—some dehumidifiers do not come with a hose, and in those cases, you also can't just leave it running for weeks while you are away. If your dehumidifier doesn't come with a hose, make sure to buy one separately.

Sensibo Air Conditioner Remote Controls

Another way—albeit an expensive one—to combat humidity in Puerto Rico is to run your air conditioner full-time. This is not the best way to keep your home mold-free, but regardless, you will need an air conditioner in Puerto Rico, since they're necessary to keep your home at a cool, comfortable temperature, especially during the hot summer months. A good way to control your air conditioner for optimal comfort and efficiency is by using the Sensibo air conditioner remote control, which allows you to oversee and control your air conditioner from your smartphone. Whether you are in a different part of Puerto

Rico, visiting the United States, or even traveling through Asia, you can check the temperature and humidity at your home through the Sensibo app. You can even turn it on from abroad to help lower the humidity.

Thanks to a geo-location feature, the Sensibo app will also automatically turn on the air conditioner to your preferred settings when you come home, and it will automatically turn off once all synced-up phones have left the home. This feature may not be useful if not everyone in the family uses the app, however.

Other Ways to Regulate Your Home Environment When Away

If you plan to be away from Puerto Rico for a while but have someone you trust back home, such as a friend or close colleague, you could offer them a spare key and ask them to check on the humidity levels and water flow, water your plants, feed your cat, and carry out other necessary tasks. If you have a dehumidifier with a large tank but no hose, this may be a suitable workaround. Obviously, though, this can only work with someone you really trust. When you're back, take them out to a nice Puerto Rican restaurant as a thank you.

Another option for keeping your home fresh is baking soda moisture-absorbing bags, which you can hang up in closets, bathrooms, and other small spaces. These bags are a cheap, easy way to keep the clothes in your closet fresh and mold-free even when you are away for extended periods—the bags are good for up to 60 days. This option will not work for large rooms but can also be a good addition to a dehumidifier if needed.

If, despite precautions, mold still grows in your home, Puerto Rico has many high-quality mold remediation companies to save your living space.

In addition to the humidity, when you are away from your home in Puerto Rico, you must also be mindful of the mail being sent to your address. Important mail may be arriving for you, but you can't check it until you return home. To keep on top of your mail while traveling, sign up for PRelocate's virtual mailbox service. We will send you pictures of your incoming mail, and you can decide whether we should physically send it to you, open it and scan the contents to your e-mail address, shred it, or store it until you return.

Preparing for a Hurricane

Puerto Ricans know how to weather hurricanes—it's part and parcel of living in Puerto Rico. However, if you're from a place where hurricanes aren't a big risk, you may not know proper hurricane preparation procedures. If you're planning to make Puerto Rico your home, here's what you should know to protect yourself, your family, and your home during a Puerto Rico hurricane.

Be Aware of Storms During Hurricane Season

Technically, Puerto Rico's hurricane season runs from June through November, but most hurricanes take place between August and October. The National Oceanic and Atmospheric Administration (NOAA) maintains the National Hurricane Center website which gives up-to-date information about developing storms.

Check it often during hurricane season and have a plan to evacuate or shelter in place long before a storm is bearing down. Keep a NOAA weather radio and extra batteries in your emergency kit.

Buy a Generator and Stock up on Gas

There's a good possibility you'll lose electricity if a hurricane strikes, and it may take several days before power is restored. Buy the smallest possible generator that will meet your needs—most people only need something to power a fan, charge a few devices, and keep a small refrigerator cold.

Remember to follow the directions for safe generator use; never plug your generator directly into the wall to avoid backfeed that may injure powerline workers.

Don't forget to keep enough gas on hand to fuel your generator for several days. It's a good idea to keep 8 to 10 gallons on hand in case fuel trucks can't get to your part of the island to restock local gas stations.

Prepare an Emergency Supplies Kit

In addition to a three-day supply of water and non-perishable food per person, the Federal Emergency Management Agency (FEMA) reminds everyone to remember these other essentials:

- Devices to communicate with family either by phone or email
- A seven-day supply of any daily medications you take
- First-aid kit
- Pet food and other necessary pet supplies
- Birth certificates, passports, and other critical documents (stored in a waterproof container)
- Matches, flashlights, and a multi-tool with can opener
- Trash bags, bathroom tissue, and other hygiene supplies
- Sleeping bag or blanket and pillow
- Books, cards, or other items to help pass the time
- Irreplaceable items you cannot afford to lose

Of course, this is a non-exhaustive list. We have a further list of important actions you should take to keep yourself safe during a hurricane in Puerto Rico:

- Fill your bathtub with water. Your water supply is likely to be cut off during a hurricane, and filling your bathtub with water gives you a supply for flushing the toilet and other applications for non-potable water.
- Harness the power of the sun: Keep the lights on with solar-powered lights. Solar-powered fans are also a good way to keep cool during a summertime hurricane. A solar mosquito zapper will also keep things bug-free as you weather the storm.
- Get a generator. You'll have to shell out some money for this, but you don't need a huge one—just get a small one that will allow you to power the fridge, a fan, and other essentials.
- Freeze water bottles. They double as ice packs and can help keep your food cold if the power goes out.
- Buy earplugs. If there are a bunch of generators in your area running, you might find it difficult to sleep without earplugs.
- Stock up on batteries—you don't know how long you'll be without power.
- Get and charge a power bank to keep your phone charged. In a power outage, mobile data on your cell phone will be your only means to connect with the wider world, and it may be important to contact friends and family or access information.
- Buy a battery-powered radio to keep up with important news, announcements, and warnings.

Keep a Go-Bag in Case You Need to Evacuate

Each member of your family should have his or her own bag; a backpack or drawstring nylon bag are good options. Have a change of clothes, daily medications, device chargers, and copies of their birth certificate or ID and insurance cards.

If you're the head of your household, keep copies of everyone's documents in your go-bag. Buy a flash drive and store photos of all your household possessions in case you need to file an insurance claim later. It's a good idea to scan all your family's important records and documents, as well, such as medical and vaccination records, passports, and Social Security cards. If you own your home, scan your deed or title documents.

Keep a week's worth of cash on hand at a minimum. When the power goes out, credit and debit cards are useless. After the storm ends, banks may limit the daily amount of cash you can withdraw for a while, so make sure you have cash to cover your needs.

Stay Safe After the Storm

If you evacuated, don't re-enter your home until it has been inspected and declared safe. The electrical lines and sewer system may be damaged.

Throw away any food in your fridge and any other foodstuffs exposed to floodwater. It's better to be overly cautious and throw away anything you're not sure about. Don't drink tap water until you know it's safe. Boil it or use a purifying system if you don't have bottled water on hand.

Floodwater is packed with germs and bacteria. Use an alcohol-based hand sanitizer if you come in contact with it. Thoroughly disinfect any surfaces in your home affected by the flood.

Follow the government's warnings about flooded roads; avoid and report any downed power lines.

Protect Against Insects

Bug populations multiply in the standing water after a hurricane. The Centers for Disease Control and Prevention (CDC) recommends using insect repellent with DEET to protect against floodwater mosquitoes.

Use a product such as Mosquito Dunks on any standing water near your home to kill mosquito larvae.

Be prepared for an explosion of fire ants after a hurricane. These nasty ants are actually waterproof and flock together for survival in a flood. Wear cuffed gloves, rubber boots, and long pants when you're cleaning standing water in your yard in case you run into a fire ant colony.

Final Thoughts

Hurricane season in Puerto Rico is stressful, but you can do a lot to secure yourself and your property if you stay informed and prepared. Have your evacuation route planned in advance and keep your car's gas tank at least half full during the season. It's also a good idea to have life vests for every member of your family, including your pets.

Registering to Vote

Even though Puerto Rico is a U.S. territory, Puerto Ricans don't vote in U.S. elections. The island has its own government, elected by the people of Puerto Rico. As a U.S. citizen from one of the 50 states, you retain the right to submit a ballot in U.S. elections even when abroad, but we recommend giving up your right to vote in the United States and registering to vote in Puerto Rico instead, as that can help you pass the closer connections test needed to establish bona fide residency in Puerto Rico.

Absentee Voting

Even if you plan to be away from Puerto Rico during an election, you might still be able to vote, as long as you register for absentee voting. To register, you have to present Bring ID and your birth certificate or passport to prove that you are a U.S. citizen, and provide the last four digits of your Social Security number and your physical and postal address in person at your local Junta De Inscripción Permanente (JIP) office or via email to the Absentee Vote Administrative Board. Use the absentee voting request form to apply.

Absentee voting privileges are only offered in specific cases—you will not be able to vote in Puerto Rican elections if you are simply vacationing abroad. The following people may vote via an absentee ballot:

- People studying in full-time programs at an accredited university or college outside of Puerto Rico
- Members of the United States Armed Forces, Coast Guard, Public Health Service, or the NOAA on active duty outside of Puerto Rico
- Members of the National Guard of Puerto Rico on active duty outside of Puerto Rico
- Contractors sponsored by the Puerto Rico Department of Labor Agriculture Employment Program who will be working outside of Puerto Rico on election day
- People stationed outside of Puerto Rico in diplomatic service of the U.S. government
- People stationed outside of Puerto Rico serving in U.S. foreign aid programs
- People stationed outside of Puerto Rico in a personnel interchange program between the Puerto Rican government and a foreign government
- Spouses, children, and other dependent relatives who live with an eligible absentee voter in any of the above categories and who are otherwise eligible to vote

- Athletes and support personnel representing Puerto Rico in sports competitions on election day
- Employees of the Puerto Rican government outside of Puerto Rico on an official trip
- Commercial airline crew members working outside of Puerto Rico on election day
- Professionals and their families who live in Puerto Rico but have been temporarily staying abroad for no more than 11 months for work or study
- Inmates who have been referred to a penal institution out of Puerto Rico
- Residents of Puerto Rico whose employer requires them to perform lawful work or services of any kind outside of Puerto Rico
- People who are receiving medical treatment, or people who are accompanying relatives or others who are receiving medical treatment, outside of Puerto Rico on the election day

Services in Puerto Rico

Doctors

Concierge Doctors in Puerto Rico

No matter where in the world you live, access to high-quality health care is a must. If you're a bona fide resident of Puerto Rico, don't fret—all across Puerto Rico are great concierge doctors and medical professionals who can offer reliable, high-quality health care to decree holders of any of Puerto Rico's many tax incentives. In Puerto Rico, you can access health care via in-person visits, online consultations, and more. Here are some of the top concierge doctors and healthcare providers in Puerto Rico.

PR Concierge & Internal Medicine Services

PR Concierge & Internal Medicine Services offers, as the name suggests, concierge and internal medicine services in Puerto Rico. The company focuses on providing you with the care you need in a comfortable and friendly environment. You can contact a medical professional anytime via phone, text, or email, and the company offers its own basic medical coverage.

Pravan Clinic

Pravan Clinic is a concierge medical services provider focused on providing high-quality healthcare services in a timely manner. The company can extend its operating hours to accommodate patients when necessary and may offer a home visit for urgent matters. You can often get an appointment on the same or next day. The company's healthcare professionals can also help you craft a nutrition and wellness plan to optimize your health.

Medical Concierge Puerto Rico

Medical Concierge Puerto Rico's mission is to provide high-quality, personalized medical care at their prestigious Condado location. The company offers personalized medical services and consultations via text, valet parking services, and unlimited home delivery of medication at no additional cost. They reach out to members on a regular basis to check in with them and make sure they're staying healthy.

Medical Concierge Puerto Rico

Medical Concierge Puerto Rico is a medical concierge company that focuses on medical and dental procedures in Puerto Rico. While it is available for Puerto Rican residents, it's also a good option for your friends back in the United

States, as it specializes in facilitating medical tourism to Puerto Rico, where the costs for procedures are significantly lower. The company covers a wide range of medical procedures, from ophthalmology to cardiology and gynecology and even cosmetics, as well as an array of dental procedures, such as implants, bridges, root canals, and surgery.

Collazo Eye

Collazo Eye is a concierge medical services provider for optometry and ophthalmology. Signing up for their program gets you access to preventative care, a free annual refraction exam, and free unlimited telemedicine consultations, which normally cost $250 to $300 per session because most health plans don't cover them. Members are also guaranteed to get an appointment for non-urgent matters within a week.

Doctors on Call

Doctors on Call is a concierge medical services provider ready to serve members via office, home, and even hotel visits. In addition to annual checkups and screening tests, the company offers medical health certifications, home care follow-up, and long-term nursing care coordination. Walk-ins are welcome.

Concierge Medical Services

Concierge Medical Services provides medical care to members whenever and in whatever form they require, whether it's walk-in care for an urgent matter, a home call, or a telemedicine consultation. Founded by leading medicine concierge services provider Dr. Javier Torres Marín, CMS's team of doctors can adjust their schedules to accommodate you ASAP if you so require.

Dr Now Puerto Rico

Dr Now Puerto Rico is a medical concierge services provider focused on bringing top-quality care to you, whether you're at home, in the office, at a hotel, or anywhere else. Care for urgent matters is available 24/7, and the company also offers preventative medical services, chronic health condition management, and annual checkups, among other services.

Generalists

If you have a minor concern or aren't sure what type of specialist you need, there are plenty of skilled general doctors in Puerto Rico. If you're a woman, MEDChic may also be worth checking out. This women's health clinic focuses on maternal and gynecological care, including adolescents, and even offers minor surgery and contraception.

Pediatricians

If you're bringing along your kids to Puerto Rico, don't fret—there are tons of great pediatricians in Puerto Rico. Kids in Puerto Rico can enjoy a high level of healthcare with good health outcomes.

Obstetrician-Gynecologists

Women's health is also a priority in Puerto Rico. If you're looking for top-quality OBGYNs, you can easily find them in Puerto Rico. Puerto Rico's skilled OBGYNs will help ensure smooth pregnancies and reliable care for all women's health issues.

Dermatologists

If you're looking for skin specialists, Puerto Rico has you covered in this area too. Puerto Rico's top dermatologists are ready to help you keep your skin smooth, healthy, and beautiful.

Dentists

Proper tooth and oral care are important for everyone. Puerto Rico dentists believe that too, which is why they work hard to provide the best dental care to all patients.

Internal Medicine

Internal medicine is a complicated medical specialty dealing with internal diseases that may be too complex for single-organ specialists to handle. Internists work with diseases that affect multiple organs or patients with several comorbidities, making them true medical experts.

Others

Of course, you can find all sorts of other medical specialists across Puerto Rico, from orthopedists and endocrinologists to psychiatrists and chiropractors. Whatever kind of medical care you need in Puerto Rico, you can likely find the right specialist for you. If you want a complete list of the island's top medical professionals, please email us at info@relocatepuertorico.com.

Insurance Providers in Puerto Rico

The insurance you have in your home state won't necessarily cover you in Puerto Rico, especially given that Puerto Rico is a territory, not a state. Nonetheless, there are plenty of insurance options you can take advantage of while enjoying life as a bona fide Puerto Rican resident. In fact, changing your insurance provider and doctors can even contribute to the establishment of bona fide residency by helping you satisfy the closer connections test requirements. We've compiled a list of some of Puerto Rico's best insurance providers here.

Health Insurance

Here are four good options if you're looking for health insurance in Puerto Rico:

- Triple-S
- Humana
- First Medical
- Auxilio Plan de Socios

Each provider offers different plans and services. Triple-S, for example, covers a large number of healthcare procedures in their direct plan. The provider also offers an app called TeleConsultaMD, available for iOS and Android, that allows users to connect with a medical professional for an online consultation any day of the week between 6 a.m. and 10 p.m.

Triple-S also has a prescription medication delivery app to allow users to easily and conveniently receive their medication without leaving the house. Triple-S members may have their prescription medications delivered right to their home at no cost.

The four health insurance providers listed above are only valid for Puerto Rico, although Triple-S does offer coverage of emergency services in the United States, as long as the U.S. provider is part of the Blue Cross Blue Shield group. If you're looking for health insurance that can cover you in both Puerto Rico and the 50 states, you only have two options. The first is the HealthShare plan from Liberty, a community-based health insurance plan where members cover each other's medical expenses. Plans are relatively cheap, but there are limits on how much a member can claim.

The second option for health insurance valid in both Puerto Rico and the United States is MCS Puerto Rico. This is a health insurance plan from the 20/22 Act Society, a society created by and for the recipients of Puerto Rico's many tax incentives. You don't need to join the 20/22 Act Society to sign up for the MCS health insurance plan, but membership does come with several additional benefits for decree holders of Puerto Rico tax incentives. In addition to health insurance, membership offers guidance through any troubles you may encounter in Puerto Rico.

Additionally, if you are an employer, perhaps for an Export Services business, and are looking for a reliable Puerto Rican health insurance plan for your employees, Humana, Triple-S, and MCS are good options.

Other Insurance

There's more in life that requires insurance than just health, although health may be the most important. You may also require home, business, car, life, motorcycle, or another type of insurance.

No matter what type of insurance you need, Puerto Rican insurance providers are here to help. Here are three Puerto Rican providers that offer various types of insurance, depending on your needs:

- Universal Group
- Seguros Multiples
- MAPFRE

Insurance is important to ensure that even if disaster strikes, you have the necessary resources and support to get back up on your feet. We, too, are dedicated to providing you with the necessary resources and information to make your move to Puerto Rico a successful one.

Using Notary Services in Puerto Rico

There are numerous processes involved in making the move to Puerto Rico to take advantage of the island's generous Act 60 tax incentives, and your dealings with the government certainly won't end just because you hold a tax incentive decree in Puerto Rico. This is especially true if you choose to open an Export Services business on the island. Many Act 60 decree holders require the services of a notary for various purposes in both Puerto Rico and the United States, and if you require notary services for a document to be used in the United States, there's a useful "notary hack" you can use.

The Hassle of Obtaining Notary Services

Notary services are a necessary evil—no one likes the burdensome process of obtaining them, but they are often necessary for interactions with the government and other legal entities. The first difficulty comes in securing an appointment, since notaries, as legal professionals, typically have their hands full with other responsibilities and may not have the time or desire to notarize your document. Once you find a notary with enough time to give you an appointment in a reasonable amount of time, prepare the necessary fee in cash—most notaries only accept cash.

If you're looking for a U.S. notary, the challenges are amplified in Puerto Rico, as U.S. notaries are extremely difficult to find locally. This can turn the seemingly simple task of having your document notarized into a never-ending journey.

Online Notary Services

If you're in Puerto Rico (or even if you're in the United States), the easiest way to notarize a document for use in the United States is through an online notary service like Notarize.

The process is easy. Users simply upload their document to the website or mobile app and fill it out using Notarize's user-friendly form completion tool. Upon completion, they must undergo an identity verification process that involves entering the last four digits of their Social Security number and answering several security questions. After that, users must submit a photograph of their ID, and once Notarize verifies it, users are connected with a Notarize agent who conducts a visual verification test by comparing the photographed ID with the person in the call. The notary asks a few questions to ensure the user is of sound mind, and after only a few minutes, the notarization is complete.

Using online notary services makes notarization quicker and easier than ever. Instead of spending hours looking for a notary, getting an appointment, and driving out to the notary's location, you can have your documents notarized in the comfort of your own home in less than 10 minutes.

Keep in mind that your Puerto Rico address will not work with Notarize—you must use a recent U.S. address. Notarize's knowledge-based authentication system uses the submitted name, address, date of birth, and last four digits of a Social Security number to generate security questions based on information from public records, and the system only works with state addresses.

Notarization in Puerto Rico

While online notary services can be a godsend for anyone who needs to quickly notarize a document for use in the United States, in general, Puerto Rico does not recognize online notarizations. Notarize allows users to easily notarize documents for use in the United States from Puerto Rico, but if you need to notarize a document for use in Puerto Rico, you will often have to find a local notary for an in-person notarization. If you're ever unsure, call the institution beforehand to confirm.

Living in Puerto Rico

Puerto Rican Culture and Lifestyle

Puerto Rico is known for its rich culture in addition to its warm weather and sunny beaches. Puerto Rico's generous tax incentives entice thousands of Americans to make the move to the island, but they often end up falling in love with the year-round pleasant weather and Caribbean lifestyle as well.

Demographics

The island has been occupied for over 500 years, with the first four hundred years under Spanish rule. For more than 100 years, Puerto Rico has been an American territory. Puerto Ricans proudly represent their unique ethnic and cultural combination of Spanish, African, and American descendants.

As of April 2020, the U.S. Census Bureau estimated a population of 3.285 million people living in Puerto Rico (down from 3.337 million in 2017).

Physical Proximity

Puerto Rico is nestled in the eastern region of the Caribbean Sea, about 1,000 miles southeast of Miami, making it a short 2 ½ hour flight. Its capital, San Juan, is located on the north coast. The island of Puerto Rico measures 100 miles long by 35 miles wide, and is known for its interior mountains which descend to coastal plains.

Puerto Rico is the easternmost and smallest island of the Greater Antilles, which also includes Cuba and Jamaica.

Infrastructure and Travel

Getting around the island by car is a breeze, as the major cities in Puerto Rico interconnect through a modern highway system that covers over 5,000 miles.

Flying to and from Puerto Rico is easy, much easier than any other nation in the Caribbean. Puerto Rico offers three airports:

- Luis Muñoz Marín International Airport in Carolina (SJU)
- Rafael Hernández Airport in Aguadilla (BQN)
- Mercedita Airport in Ponce (PSE)

All three airports offer direct flights to and from the U.S. mainland.

The main airport is Luis Muñoz Rivera International Airport (SJU) in San Juan; it is the hub of the region and provides service to over 17 cities in the United States, plus more points in the Caribbean, North America, South America, and Europe. The airport attracts over 10 million passengers annually, generating the most air traffic in the Caribbean.

San Juan also offers the largest cruise ship and cargo port in the Eastern Caribbean; more than 1.78 million cruise ship passengers sail to and from San Juan each year.

Restaurants

There are a variety of food options in Puerto Rico. The staples include rice and beans but there are a variety of restaurants around San Juan especially that offer a variety of different cuisines. Puerto Rican food I a fusion of Latin American and European food styles with native Puerto Rican twists. Pork and chicken are two of the most popular meats on the island and are often thoroughly spiced. Coffee is a staple for breakfast on the island which is usually a smaller meal while dinner is often heavy. Weet and sour combinations are popular in lunch and dinner meals in Puerto Rico and the creativity with which Puerto Ricans approach meals keeps them interesting.

Typically, San Juan has a wider variety of places to eat along with traditional Puerto Rican meals. If you are craving food from a different culture, you can almost certainly find it.

Resorts and Nightlife

Puerto Rico offers an extensive list of places to stay in and relax or go out on the town and party. One of the more popular places to stay in the San Juan area is Dorado Beach, which is a luxury beach resort which allows people to experience the highlights of Caribbean life with numerous amenities. Old San Juan has a variety of boutique hotels as well which are great places to stay or go get drinks on your way out to the explore the town. If you find yourself at a nightclub in Puerto Rico, be sure to expect lots of high energy dancing and lively music. One of the more famous spots to go out in Puerto Rico is La Placita de Santurce. It is a marketplace with restaurants by day and an outdoor club by night. Historically, the place was a two-tiered market square offering a variety of produce and necessities, but now it has become one of Santurce's top nightlight venues. The square features kiosks that sell beloved Puerto Rican fried foods such as empanadillas, and from Thursday until Sunday, you can enjoy live music, ranging from salsa, to jazz, to rock, and can even enjoy some karaoke.

Outdoor Activities

If you have come to Puerto Rico and want to explore the natural beauty of the Caribbean Island, you have a plethora of options. The El Yunque National Forest is the only tropical rainforest in the United States Department of Agriculture's (USDA) forest system. Although it spans only 29,000 acres, this national treasure is one of the most biologically diverse forests in the USDA forest system, with many plant and animal species not found in any other USDA forest. Twenty-four miles of hiking trails stretch through the forest and are open for adventurers and their leashed dogs to explore. Other activities in Puerto Rico include surfing, parasailing, skydiving, fishing, and more.

General Economic Status of Puerto Rico

Despite the island's fervent efforts to implement curfews, quarantines, and mask mandates, COVID-19 made its impact on Puerto Rico in 2020. The GDP dropped 7.5 percent. The pandemic further highlighted the island's economic and social issues that Hurricane Maria and recent earthquakes exacerbated. However, the International Monetary Fund's April 2021 report predicts an estimated growth of 2.5 percent and 0.7 percent in 2021 and 2022, respectively. Hurricane Maria devastated the island's economy and left it with a crippling debt with 71.5 billion in bonds and 50 billion in pension bonds. Unemployment rates have also risen in the wake of COVID-19 and are expected to increase to 9.6 percent in 2021. In the post Hurricane Maria life on the island, approximately 46 percent of the island lives under the poverty line.

COVID-19 and recent natural disasters have had a tremendous impact on the Puerto Rican economy. However, the money brought in by Act 60 has had a positive impact on the economy. Wages generated from Act 20 businesses generated almost $26 million in direct fiscal revenues from 2015 to 2019. Further, total investments have grown from almost $500 million in 2015-2016 to over $1.2 billion.

Considering its placement in the Caribbean, Puerto Rico is heavily dependent upon imports but its arable land is one of the most important natural resources on the island. Sugar cane, coffee, pineapple, plantains, and animal products are produced on the island. Most of the land on the island is fertile but not used. Potential investors looking for an industry in which to invest should research the potential of cultivating the agriculture industry on the island which has been overlooked in recent years. Additionally, as Puerto Rico has moved away from industrial production and toward a capital-based service industry, this has proven to be a stable move in a place where tropical life can be unpredictable.

Different Taxation

Puerto Rican citizens are treated to special consideration by the United States. Even though Puerto Ricans are American citizens, any income which is realized on the island by a bona fide Puerto Rico resident is excluded from U.S. federal income taxation (as explained in U.S. Code Section 933). This income is instead taxed at Puerto Rico local rates, which may be significantly lower.

As of 2017, individual income tax brackets ranged from 0% to 33%, while corporations are taxed at a rate of 39%, which drops as low as 4% with Act 60. Equally important to note is that self-employed individuals pay self-employment taxes, which includes both Social Security and Medicare taxes, and are eligible for federal retirement benefits.

It is important to understand "bona fide residence" as defined for income tax purposes.

Local Economy

Puerto Rico is recognized for its diversified economy. It is involved in a variety of important manufacturing industries, such as clothing, textiles, processed foods, pharmaceuticals, petrochemicals, and electronics. It is estimated that manufacturing produces more than 40% of its GDP.

The service sector has also grown noticeably in recent years. Key employers in education and health, professional and business industries, and financial and insurance services have benefited greatly from the local workforce.

The World Bank reports Puerto Rico generated $103 billion in gross domestic product (GDP) in 2020. With a population of 3.285 million citizens in 2020, this works out to a GDP per capita exceeding $30,000.

The top nations importing goods from Puerto Rico are: the United States (68%), Germany (8%), the Netherlands (5%), and Belgium (4%). These nations are typically purchasing pharmaceutical goods, medicines, medical equipment and supplies, computers and electronics, and food items.

When it comes to purchasing exports, Puerto Rico is buying goods from: the United States (51%), Ireland (16%), Singapore (5%), and Japan (4%). Puerto Rico generally buys energy products (petroleum and coal), chemicals, pharmaceuticals, medicines, and food products.

Recently, Puerto Rico's debt of $70 billion has been somberly announced on the evening news, often in conjunction with damages caused by Hurricane Maria. What is usually omitted from the conversation is the fact that Puerto Rico continues to work through this with their fiscal austerity program, managed by the PROMESA oversight board.

USD Currency

Puerto Rico uses the U.S. dollar and operates under the U.S. monetary policy system. It falls under the purview of the Federal Reserve Bank of New York, one of the 12 Federal Reserve Banks.

Convention Center

The island is proud to boast its own convention center. It is the largest convention center in the Caribbean and the most technologically advanced space found throughout the Caribbean and Latin America. With 580,000 square feet of usable space, the Center hosts crowds exceeding 10,000 people.

Entity

Just like the United States, Puerto Rico accepts standard methods of business ownership, including sole proprietorships and general partnerships and extending to special purpose corporate forms and limited liability companies. This gives investors enough choices to create an effective liability shield and take advantage of preferential tax incentives and breaks.

Puerto Rican Politics

Government

As a U.S. commonwealth, Puerto Rico is governed by the U.S. federal system and guided by U.S. federal and local laws. While Puerto Rico follows the U.S. Constitution, this independent territory created its own constitution. They enforce their own laws and regulations, so long as they do not conflict with federal laws. Puerto Rico's local government functions similarly to other U.S. states, with executive, legislative, and judicial branches functioning interdependently.

Since Puerto Rico is a commonwealth instead of an American state, different rights are conferred upon its citizens. For instance, persons born in Puerto Rico are citizens of the United States but are not granted the right to vote in presidential elections, although they can vote in presidential primaries. Puerto Rican citizens do not need a passport to enter or leave mainland United States, but international visitors arriving to the island from outside the United States must present their passports for admission.

Understanding the General Elections

Although Puerto Rico is a U.S. territory, its political system is almost entirely separate from that of the mainland United States. Puerto Rican residents vote in local elections for their mayors, representatives, senators, and governor and *not* in U.S. federal elections. U.S. expats who relocate to Puerto Rico—say, for its lucrative tax incentives—have the choice of renouncing their right to vote in U.S. elections and registering to vote in Puerto Rico. For Act 60 decree holders, this is highly recommended because it helps fulfill the requirements of the "closer connection" test for bona fide Puerto Rican residency.

Puerto Rican Political Parties

Unlike the mainland United States, which features only the Democrats and the Republicans as the two primary parties, Puerto Rico has three traditional parties: the Partido Popular Democrático (PPD), the Partido Nuevo Progresista (PNP), and Partido Independentista Puertorriqueño (PIP). Liberals and conservatives can be found in both the PPD and the PNP, but the PPD tends to have more liberals, and the PNP tends to have more conservatives.

One of the key defining points of Puerto Rican parties is where they stand on the issue of Puerto Rican sovereignty. The PPD was founded in the 1930s and is in favor of maintaining the status quo of Puerto Rico as a Commonwealth territory. The PNP, conversely, was founded in 1967 and believes Puerto Rico should be a U.S. state. The PIP, founded in 1946, is the strongest advocate for Puerto Rican independence, and although it has never won a gubernatorial election, several of its members have served in Congress.

In the 2020 election, three additional parties also ran for governor: Projecto Dignidad, Movimiento Victoria Ciudadana, and Movimiento de Conciencia. Though these parties do not make clear their stance on Puerto Rican statehood, they generally lean strongly toward independence. Movimiento Victoria Ciudadana proposes a constitutional assembly to make a final determination on Puerto Rico's relationship with the United States, and Movimiento de Conciencia advocates for self-sufficiency on the island, especially in agriculture and manufacturing.

Natural Disasters on the Island

Natural disasters may create an additional 14 days for Act 60 decree holders to count toward being on the island for the Presence Test even if they were on the mainland during the allotted period. Act 60 decree holders must be on the island for 183 days per year in order to meet bona fide residency requirements.

However, while additional presence days can help Act 60 decree holders satisfy the Presence Test, living in Puerto Rico 183 days a year is not enough to automatically be considered a bona fide resident. Instead, Act 60 decree holders must also satisfy the tax home and closer connection tests.

Hurricane Maria's Impact on the Island

In September 2017 when Hurricane Maria, following on the heels of Hurricane Irma, directly hit the island of Puerto Rico and devastated this U.S. territory and popular vacation destination. Hurricane Maria is on record as the worst natural disaster to strike Puerto Rico, with an official death toll of 2,975, and over $94 billion in damage.

Hurricane Maria Damage Summary

With winds increasing from 85 mph to 165 mph in a 24-hour period and directly striking Puerto Rico, this Category 4 storm gained the upper hand, wiping out structures and the electrical grid for almost the entire island. The damage was unavoidable and extensive.

Equally destructive was the downpour of rain accompanying the raging winds. Some areas experienced as much as 38 inches of rainfall; the La Plata River quickly overran its watershed. The northern part of the island was affected the most by the flooding. The capital, San Juan, was flooded throughout; in some areas, water was waist-deep and many structures lost their roofs.

Just two weeks prior to the landing of Maria, Hurricane Irma had already left about 80,000 residents without power when Maria hit the shores. The power grid, which was already stressed and fragile, was destroyed, eliminating power throughout the entire island. A week later, when experts were finally able to make a reasonable assessment, it was determined that 95% of the population had no power or cell phone service. Almost half the population did not have access to drinking water.

The agricultural industry was also hit hard. Hurricane Maria wiped out 80% of the island's crops, with losses tagged at $780 million and necessitating a shift toward imported fresh produce, creating another unexpected expense. Another industry directly affected by the storm was tourism. Puerto Rico was not officially announced as reopened until the middle of December 2017, three months after Maria left her destructive mark. Even then, tourism got off to a slow and tentative start, as many travelers were hesitant, uncertain about how much damage remained and whether it would limit their activities and enjoyment.

Initial Recovery Process

As is common with network news cycles, tragedy and outrage attract viewers. For most Americans, the first stages of recovery in Puerto Rico were fraught with confusion, incompetence, and even nightmarish tales of stranded citizens left to their own devices. On a nightly basis, the lack of electricity and drinking water was broadcast alongside reports of mounting repair costs and the precarious state of the island's finances with little attention or mention of any positive actions or progress being made.

Meanwhile, on the ground in Puerto Rico, recovery work was already underway. Considering the immensity of this storm and the widespread destruction and debris, the initial startup was slow. Supplies had to be flown in and generators set up in key areas to kickstart repairs.

As other, more urgent and topical news shoved the woes of Puerto Rico into the background, sporadic reports indicated that recovery was taking longer than it should. For instance, one month after the tragedy, 88% of the residents still had no power. Three months after Maria, 45% of the population was still without power. What was not clarified was that most of those unfortunate residents lived outside major cities of Puerto Rico.

Current Status of Recovery Efforts After Hurricane Maria

It is impressive what a little time and a lot of energy can do, and important to see how Puerto Rico quickly recovered from the historical hurricane Maria after it wreaked havoc on the island in late 2017. Only by May 2019, the lingering damage caused by the hurricane in most large cities like San Juan were already minimal and fading fast into the background.

Many major resorts and restaurants in San Juan smartly took advantage of the unfortunate and widespread damage to perform upgrades, redesigns, and improvements on their properties. Visitors to San Juan these days find it thriving and vibrant; merchants are happy to be back in business and residents have bounced back energetically and positively.

It is not as if Puerto Ricans have never seen storm damage before. Granted, no one had witnessed damage such as Maria wreaked in 2017, but the attitude seems to be that it will just take a little longer to get back on their feet after this whopper struck them — and this sentiment was right.

While in December 2017 almost half the island was waiting for power to turn back on, by mid-2018, almost 99% of the island had electricity again. Although there have been many complaints about U.S. assistance, Puerto Rico gratefully accepted any help that came its way.

The Army Corps of Engineers was given its marching orders to pack up and leave after spending over $2 billion restoring power to the island. With 1,000 contractors and 1,200 personnel working on the island, the Corps of Engineers planted over 52,000 power poles and threaded over 5,700 miles of wire crisscrossing Puerto Rico in less than a year. Another proactive response to this disaster recovery was to install solar panels across the island and connecting them to generators.

Although by May 2019, blue tarps still served as roofs for some buildings, especially in more isolated areas, most of the debris had been cleaned up. Most roads were already clear, so driving around Puerto Rico was viable and safe.

By 2021, the island has essentially fully recovered with thriving economic activities of all industries. The remnants of hurricane Maria are few to be seen.

How Prepared is Puerto Rico?

Before Hurricane Maria, Puerto Rico's preparedness plan for the hurricane season was intended to withstand Category 1 storms, what the island is used to dealing with. Because Maria came hard and fast and ripped the island to shreds, extensive damage was unavoidable. That also brought the sobering realization that their readiness program needed serious overhauling, which is what the government has done.

FEMA has strategically situated four warehouses on the island, a huge improvement over the single warehouse that was in place when Maria landed. These buildings are stocked with thousands of tarps, as well as millions of bottles of water and emergency meals. On top of that foundation of security, FEMA sought to directly supply each municipality in Puerto Rico, giving mayors enough basic resources to immediately distribute essentials to their own community in case another horrendous storm isolates them.

The communications infrastructure also received a crucial boost with the burying of more than 1,000 miles of fiber cable underground in place of putting up new power poles that could easily collapse again from another Category 3 or 4 storm. Additionally, critical facilities (hospitals, fire departments, and police stations) are installing satellite systems with over 300 hospitals also getting new radio antennas.

The biggest worry is the power grid. As it is still not fully repaired, there have been two island-wide blackouts since full restoration, one from a falling tree and another from an excavator accidentally hitting a power line. The good news is that power is restored with little delay, so it is more of an inconvenience than a new hazard for the residents who have faced enough problems from the aftermath of Maria.

As an extra safety net, FEMA is leaving 700 emergency generators behind along with three massive generators that were installed at the major power plants in Puerto Rico.

The biggest unknown in the preparedness plan is the force and strength of storms Puerto Rico will encounter during future hurricane seasons. If another storm of the intensity of Maria hits, it will not be easy, but it will certainly be less dreadful than the debacle of 2017. If, as everyone hopes, Puerto Rico faces just typical storm seasons, the island should be well equipped to weather any storms with nominal damage.

Puerto Rico's Economy After Hurricane Maria

A year after hurricane Maria hit the island, Puerto Rico actively looked forward to rebuilding its tourist industry in 2018. Within a year San Juan was already hopping again. For travelers who wanted to avoid crowds, there was no better time to take advantage of the fun and beauty of San Juan than 2018. With most shops open for business in the capital, there were plenty of choices for the selective wanderer to pick from.

As for hotels, many locations were still making repairs and may had fewer rooms open to the public. Nonetheless, the city of San Juan was operating as usual. While tourists may saw some scars from Maria, much of the city was back to its usual good food, tropical weather, and excellent friends, only one year after the natural disaster.

For an alternative to traditional hotel stays, Airbnb was active throughout Puerto Rico in 2018. Even better, they were stepping up to the plate and displaying a generous spirit in their effort to encourage tourists to enjoy and support Puerto Rico. In 2018, any Airbnb Experience or stay in Puerto Rico directly benefitted the island as Airbnb donated 100% of those commissions to local nonprofit agencies dedicated to assisting in Puerto Rico's recovery.

Millions of people helped Puerto Rico directly or by supporting foundations and groups involved with the recovery efforts. For instance, United for Puerto Rico received over $39 million in donations, much of it from tourists in 2018.

As of November 2021, Puerto Rico fully has recovered and the island is bustling with life and fun like never before.

Statehood for Puerto Rico

Is it possible that Puerto Rico will become the 51st U.S. state? Overwhelming results from a non-binding referendum vote in 2020 suggests that many Puerto Ricans are in favor of becoming a state. However, for the referendum in question only 54% of eligible citizens voted. This low turnout along with other considerations like U.S. politics and the Constitution, are hurdles along the road to Puerto Rico becoming a state. The conversation of Puerto Rico becoming a state often occurs in tangent with the discussion of Washington D.C. becoming a state. In June of 2021, the governor of Puerto Rico, Pedro Pierluisi, called the territory's lack of statehood "geographic discrimination."

To understand the possibility of Puerto Rico becoming a 51st state, it is important to recognize what Puerto Rico is to the United States: a commonwealth.

What Does It Mean to Be a Commonwealth?

It was in 1898, after the Spanish-American War that Puerto Rico first came under U.S. control. However, it was not until 1952 that it was officially approved under U.S. federal law, making Puerto Rico a commonwealth. For residents on the island, becoming a U.S. commonwealth meant:

- A separate constitution from the United States
- Having to pay federal income taxes on work done within the States
- Access to Medicare and Medicaid by paying into Social Security
- Not having a vote in U.S. Congress
- Having the right to vote in primary presidential elections, but not presidential elections
- Being considered natural-born U.S. citizens

After the 2016 gubernatorial elections, Puerto Rico's then new governor Ricardo Rosselló stated that voters were seeking to claim their "equal rights as American citizens." Being in a state of economic crisis, Puerto Rico filed for bankruptcy in May of 2017. It has since announced that it will try and exit its bankruptcy status by the end of 2021. Rosselló along with other statehood supporters believed that bankruptcy could help repair the island's economy.

The Process for Becoming a U.S. state

Ultimately it is up to Congress to admit new states via the "New States" clause found in the United States Constitution. As defined in a 1953 U.S. Senate Committee on Interior and Insular Affairs, the requirements for statehood are:

- The residents of the proposed new state are all for the principles of democracy as presented in the American form of government.
- The majority of the electorate wants statehood.
- The proposed new state has the population and resource to support state government and carry its share of the cost of the Federal Government.

The Puerto Rican Debt Crisis and PROMESA

After World War 2, the United States federal government wanted to restructure the Puerto Rican economy and modernize it to adapt with changing times. By 1976, Puerto Rico had largely remained an agricultural economy with remnants from its Spanish colonial past. As such, the U.S. Congress passed new tax provisions that ultimately made Puerto Rico a tax haven for large corporations wanting to avoid high taxes in mainland United States. Considering its original intentions, the law was rather successful—ultimately attracting large numbers of massive corporations to move their manufacturing facilities to the island and significantly boosting the economy.

Unfortunately, this economic growth was short-lived. In 1996, in an effort to reduce the federal tax deficit, the U.S. government repealed the tax rule that had previously given life to the Puerto Rican economy. By 2006 when the entirety of the law was phased out, virtually all of the large corporations on the island had pulled themselves off the island, putting the Puerto Rican economy on a plunging downfall until this day. In the 30 years that the law was in effect, the Puerto Rican economy depended solely upon large corporations so much that it was not able to adapt after the law was repealed. Not only that, as the U.S. economy grew in mainland United States, an overwhelming number Puerto Ricans left the island in search of better economic opportunities, further leaving Puerto Rico in economic peril and forcing the Puerto Rican government to take out large debts.

To address this debt issue, the U.S. Congress passed a bi-partisan law in 2016 called the Puerto Rico Oversight, Management, and Economic Stability Act (PROMESA). This law was aimed at restructuring Puerto Rican debt and established a Fiscal Control Board (FCB) for the island. The board is composed of seven members appointed by the President of the United States and the Governor of Puerto Rico holding ex officio membership without voting rights. The FCB works in conjunction with the Puerto Rican government in promoting economic growth on the island and make other sound financial policies. Now, given its many new laws, tax provisions, and other good economic policies, Puerto Rico is attracting Americans from all 50 states and is destined for a bright future ahead.

General Life on the Island

While life in Puerto Rico may present some new challenges, you will be pleased to learn of the many benefits the island offers in comparison to living on the mainland United States.

Housing Choices

When it comes to selecting housing for you and your family, you have a lot of options from which to choose. If you are a city person, then the San Juan metro area will meet your needs, from modern neighborhoods to the charming European ambience found in Old San Juan, along with plenty in between.

If high-rise living with amenities next to the beach is attractive, consider an apartment in Condado. For more seclusion and security, try a gated family community in Dorado. Or immerse yourself in a bohemian lifestyle, popular with the local crowd in Ocean Park. Just like in the United States, there are many ways to enjoy life on Puerto Rico.

Both renters and homeowners are likely to be impressed at the rates and prices of properties in Puerto Rico. For instance, a recent Zillow search on Puerto Rico rentals revealed 2 bedroom/2 bath homes in good areas with average rents of $1,500 per month. At times, you might see price volatility, like when there are fewer renovated units for rent or when hurricanes affect supply and demand.

Education System

Parents will be delighted to learn that public and private schools are numerous, and many shine in comparison to U.S. city school systems.

For families preferring private education, outstanding choices abound, including private schools with religious training. It should also be noted that many private schools find their students in high demand at top rated U.S. universities. Check out Saint John's School, which is popular in the San Juan area.

There are numerous higher educational institutions, from universities and colleges to technical institutes and community colleges. The University of Puerto Rico is the largest public university on the island, where over 3,000 university degrees are granted each year. More than a third of those degrees are bestowed annually in the important areas of technology, mathematics, the sciences, and business administration.

Crime and Security Concerns

Just like major cities in mainland America, crime can and does occur in Puerto Rico. San Juan, capital of the island, is the most populous city and consequently experiences more incidents of crime than other areas. However, just as you use common sense when visiting or living in major cities on the mainland, similar care should be taken in San Juan and neighboring towns.

Utility Services

The electric grid in Puerto Rico is notoriously underdeveloped, and thanks to Hurricane Maria in 2017, has been a major topic of discussion. Maria was neither the first nor last hurricane that will hit the island, which is why many residences and businesses are prepared for power outages with backup generators. While short outages are common in metro areas, they do not significantly disrupt day-to-day living.

Puerto Rico's water and wastewater systems adhere to the same standards required by the EPA on the mainland. U.S. tap water is consumable across the entire island.

Transportation Services

You will discover hundreds of direct daily flights to and from most major U.S. cities, even as distant as Montreal or New York. San Juan International Airport (SJU) is the normal point of arrival and departure, but there are also two other passenger airports servicing other areas of the island. The map below illustrates non-stop flight destinations from SJU.

As for driving, primary road conditions are comparable to what you find on the mainland. Transportation options include taxis, buses, and Uber.

Healthcare

You will find typical U.S. standards when it comes to the local healthcare system, with quality medical facilities and physicians available. You will also find health insurance premiums are less expensive than in the United States. The best place to start looking for insurance would be to research Triple-S Salud, Puerto Rico's largest insurance provider. There are also private group "concierge style" options available.

Banking Options

As a commonwealth of the United States, U.S. banking regulations and services mirror mainland U.S. bank operations, offering similar products and protections, including FDIC protection up to $250,000. Banco Popular is the most popular bank for both personal and business purposes.

Communications

When it comes to cell phones, internet, and U.S. mail, there is little difference living on Puerto Rico.

For cell phones, you will find most U.S. carriers offering their services in Puerto Rico without additional fees. Some companies perform better in certain areas than others.

Fiber internet is available with a direct connection to the United States.

Weather

It's hard to beat Puerto Rico's climate, which is described as tropical rain forest, with yearly temperatures ranging from warm to hot and averaging 70-85 degrees F. The rainy season in Puerto Rico runs from April to November and includes the Atlantic hurricane season.

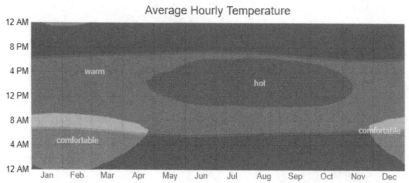

Average Hourly Temperature

Cost of Living in Puerto Rico

Cost of Living in Puerto Rico vs. Cost of Living in the United States

Living in Puerto Rico under one of its many tax incentive programs offers numerous advantages to U.S. citizens: the beautiful weather, the vibrant Caribbean lifestyle, and, of course, the comparatively low cost of living. What's really great about Puerto Rico is that the quality of life is high and residents can access state-of-the-art health care, high-speed internet, and exciting cultural experiences, all for a lower price than in the Mainland United States.

Though Puerto Rico is a U.S. territory, it has developed its own economy and laws as a Caribbean island. It is American yet offers an island paradise lifestyle with relatively low prices: in other words, it's the perfect destination for Americans looking to relocate.

Cost of Living in Puerto Rico

The cost of living varies across different regions of Puerto Rico, and the same is true for the United States. Therefore, it's impossible to give a comparison that will be accurate for all situations. Here, we'll compare the two most expensive cities in Puerto Rico and the United States—San Juan and New York City—using data pulled from Numbeo to give you a rough idea. If you are moving from a rural area to San Juan, the price differences may not be so stark, but in general, if you are moving from a U.S. city, anywhere in Puerto Rico will be considerably cheaper.

Overall, the living costs in San Juan are roughly 70% of those in New York City. Restaurant meals are much easier to afford in San Juan, with prices 30% to 50% lower. Good news for beer lovers: it's as much as 160% cheaper. Supermarket prices are also generally lower, varying depending on the food, but expect to save around 30% on your overall grocery list.

In San Juan, you can use public transportation for significantly less than in NYC—a monthly pass is nearly 300% cheaper. However, taxis, gasoline, and new cars are, surprisingly, more expensive in San Juan. Similarly, you'll have to pay more for utilities in San Juan—not everything is better.

When it comes to the most important expense, though—rent or housing prices—San Juan is clearly far superior to New York City. You're almost guaranteed to pay significantly less in San Juan for an equivalent apartment or house in New York City, with savings around 300%. In San Juan, the average three-bedroom apartment in the city center costs $1,882.14 per month, whereas it would be $6,327.67 in NYC.

The cost of living in Puerto Rico compares favorably to U.S. cities such as Orlando, FL or Austin, TX, and is 15%-30% less expensive than Miami or Seattle. When compared to expensive cities like Washington, D.C., San Francisco, or New York City, you can live 50% cheaper in Puerto Rico. Imported goods, vehicles, and electricity tend to cost more than in the U.S., but many other items including local foods, property taxes, transportation, and healthcare are more affordable on the island. To check prices on specific items in Puerto Rico, organized by categories such as food, housing, etc., this cost of living calculator is a good tool to have on hand.

Cost of living in San Juan vs. New York City

Category	Item	Puerto Rican Price ($)	U.S. Price ($)
Food	Meal, Inexpensive Restaurant	$15.00	$20.00
	Meal for 2 in fast food chain (Burger King, etc.)	$7.25	$9.00
	Pepsi (0.33 L)	$1.45	$2.14
	Water (0.33 L)	$1.15	$1.81
	Bread (1 loaf)	$2.31	$3.94
	Cheese (1 kg)	$8.24	$13.16
	Eggs (1 dozen)	$3.08	$3.16
	Milk (1 L)	$1.76	$1.20
	Boneless Chicken (1 kg)	$9.72	$13.07
	Tomatoes (1 kg)	$4.26	$6.35
	Onions (1 kg)	$2.70	$4.21
Housing	1 BR apt. in city center (cities vary)	$916.67	$3,050.50
	1 BR apt. Away from city center (cities vary)	$662.50	$2,035.12
	Internet	$61.47	$66.69
Transportation	Fuel (1 L)	$0.76	$0.77
	One-month public transport pass	$32.50	$130.00
	Taxi (1 km)	$2.00	$1.86
	New vehicle (Volkswagen Golf 1.4)	$25,000.00	$23,000.00
Childcare	One month of preschool for 1 child	$516.67	$2,566.35
Clothes	Jeans	$49.20	$62.57
	Business shoes	$98.00	$134.60
	Dress	$45.00	$47.52
Entertainment	Gym membership (monthly)	$46.00	$112.00
	Movie ticket	$8.50	$17.00
	Local beer (0.5 liter)	$3.00	$7.20

Source: Numbeo 2021

Live a Better Life in Puerto Rico

Under tax incentives like the Act 60 Export Services incentive, you can live a better life in Puerto Rico than in the Mainland United States. Businesses that qualify for the Export Services tax incentive are based in Puerto Rico but export their services overseas, meaning they can boost their income through Puerto Rico's lower cost of living, since their revenue comes from abroad. With this setup, it's easy to live a luxurious life in Puerto Rico.

Puerto Rico's low expenses are one of the main draws of people to the island—alongside, of course, its beautiful weather and vibrant culture. Everyone's situation is different, but in general, living in Puerto Rico is cheaper than living in the Mainland United States.

Puerto Rico Treasury's 7% Tax on Prepared Foods

Good news for restaurant owners and patrons in Puerto Rico—as of October 1, 2019, the Puerto Rico Treasury has cut the sales and use tax (abbreviated IVU in Spanish) on prepared foods to 7%. The tax rate is down from its previous 11.5%, saving restaurant patrons 4.5% in taxes per visit. The Treasury recognized the importance of the restaurant industry and prepared food establishments in the Puerto Rican economy in a press release, stating that these establishments demonstrated their significance in the aftermath of devastating hurricanes Irma and Maria.

The tax cut was first determined in Act 257 of 2018 of the New Tax Model, and Puerto Rico Treasury Secretary Francisco Parés Alicea worked with José Salvatella, president of the Association of Restaurants of Puerto Rico (ASORE), to discuss the requirements for the lowered tax rate. Salvatella stated that while ASORE would like to see the sales and use tax eliminated entirely for prepared foods, the organization is pleased with the benefits this tax reduction will afford consumers, restaurant businesses, and the Treasury alike.

Establishments Eligible for the Tax Cut

The tax cut applies not only to restaurants but to any commercial establishment that sells food or beverages that are hot and/or served with utensils. This means that not only restaurants but also bars, pubs, canteens, cafés, food trucks, food stands, caterers, and food service contractors can take advantage of the new 7% tax rate. It is important to note, however, that the tax cut applies only to prepared food items, carbonated beverages, candy, and pastries, and alcoholic beverages are not subject to the new rate.

Requirements for Restaurants to Charge the Lowered Tax Rate

Before they can charge the new, lower rate, restaurants and other food establishments need to possess an Authorized Business Certificate, which they must display in a visible area of the establishment to notify patrons of the lowered tax rate.

The Authorized Business Certificate is only issued to restaurants that hold a valid Merchant's Registration Certificate (MRC) within the North American Industry Classification System (NAICS) and that meet certain requirements, most notably the following:

- The merchant must be up to date on all its IVU filings and declarations.
- The merchant must not have any outstanding tax debts or be registered in a tax debt payment program.
- The merchant must own, install, and maintain an IVU terminal at all of its point-of-sale systems.

Merchants who met all the requirements were automatically granted the Authorized Business Certificate on September 23, 2019, and started charging the new rate on October 1, 2019. Every year on September 30, establishments that continue to comply to the requirements will have their certificates automatically renewed. Those who are no longer in compliance will lose their certificates and can request another certificate once they are in compliance again.

Restaurants Charging the New 7% Tax Rate

According to the Treasury Department's records, there are around 22,000 registered restaurants in Puerto Rico, but ASORE asserts that this number is misleading, given that some establishments on the list have since gone out of business or operate within a larger business, such as a small restaurant in a gas station. The number of open businesses eligible for the tax cut is significantly smaller, and the Unified Internal Revenue System (SURI)'s website lists as of this writing 7,155 locations that offer the reduced tax rate.

The search feature on SURI makes it easy for users to check for establishments, offering the ability to search by city or restaurant name. The cities are listed alphabetically, with each city featuring an alphabetically ordered list of the applicable restaurants. The list features everything from McDonald's and Burger Kings, to pizzerias, to cafés, to even hotels.

Cost of Food

The price of food is roughly the same as in the United States. The island has many supermarket chains, such as SuperMax, Pueblo, and Supermercados Econo, whose websites you can check to get an idea of what Puerto Rican supermarkets offer and what their prices are. Freshmart is a bit more expensive, but it offers organic, gluten-free products, grass-fed meats, and free-range eggs.

If you would like to buy healthy, fresh, local produce, be sure to check out Puerto Rico's many farmer's markets as well. They can be found all across the island, and Puerto Rico's tropical rainforest climate allows for a wide range of produce to be grown.

You can also find American staples such as Walmart and Costco if you're looking for something more familiar. The island has four Costco locations: Carolina, East Bayamon, West Bayamon, and Caguas. Walmarts can be found all across the island, just like any U.S. state.

Cost of Health Care

Health care is significantly cheaper in Puerto Rico than in the United States—expect to save up to 30%, depending on your current state. The standard is similar to what you would receive in the United States, although conditions do vary across the island. You will receive the highest-quality health care in San Juan.

The quality of public health care in Puerto Rico is quite high, but because the island is facing a shortage of doctors, waiting times tend to be long. It may be worth considering private health care to avoid the long wait times. Medical insurance is generally affordable, and Puerto Rican insurers are generally more likely to cover pre-existing conditions than insurers in the United States. Bear in mind, though, that some healthcare providers do not accept credit card payments, so it's a good idea to bring some cash along.

Cost of Wellness and Fitness

Puerto Rico is a great place to get—or stay—fit. There are tons of gym options around the island, particularly in San Juan, and if you get a membership at a gym like Planet Fitness or Crunch, you can spend as little as $10 per month. Another unique and affordable fitness option is Deep Lifestyle, a dance-style workout group that promotes physical and mental wellbeing. The workouts are geared toward women, but interested men are also invited to join. The island also features various wellness centers and other activities such as yoga at reasonable prices.

Cost of Transportation

One of the best ways to get around in Puerto Rico is Uber, and you can use the website to calculate the rate for your route. However, Uber is not available throughout the entire island—if you're in the southwestern quadrant, you will need to find alternative transportation.

When Uber isn't available, there are always taxis. Within San Juan, you will pay metered fares, but outside of the capital, there are typically no meters. Taxi drivers only accept cash, and don't forget to include a tip. Taxi drivers might be nicer to you if you speak Spanish, so be sure to flaunt your Spanish skills if you have any.

Of course, since you are residing in Puerto Rico long-term, it may be worth it to just buy a car. If you don't want to splurge on a new car, it's easy to find a used car to purchase in Puerto Rico. You will also need a driver's license and a "car tag" (marbete).

Security on the Island

Moving to Puerto Rico is a huge life event, and there are many things you need to take into consideration. One particularly important thing to know before your big move is the level of security in Puerto Rico. These factors may influence where on the island you choose to make your home, so comprehensive research is advisable.

For the most part, Puerto Rico is perfectly safe, so don't worry. However, there are some things you should be aware of, and you should take normal safety precautions as you would in any U.S. city.

Puerto Rico vs. the United States

One of the most important considerations when deciding where in Puerto Rico to relocate is the crime levels. When researching security in Puerto Rico, you must keep in mind that crime is found in every major city, whether in Puerto Rico or the United States. Puerto Rico, being a Caribbean island with a poor economy, often gets a bad reputation in terms of security, but in fact, 2019 FBI crime statistics reveal that the island has a lower crime rate than many U.S. states, including New York, California, and Texas.

	Violent crime	Rape	Robbery	Property crime
Puerto Rico	6,479 0.20%	215 0.01%	2,121 0.07%	22,441 0.70%
California	174,331 0.44%	14,799 0.04%	52,301 0.13%	921,114 2.33%
New York	69,764 0.36%	6,583 0.03%	18,068 0.09%	267,155 1.37%
Texas	121,474 0.42%	14,824 0.05%	28,988 1.00%	693,204 2.39%

	Puerto Rico		California		New York		Texas	
Population	3,193,694		39,512,223		19,453,561		28,995,881	
Violent crime[1]	6,479	0.20%	174,331	0.44%	69,764	0.36%	121,474	0.42%
Murder and nonnegligent manslaughter	606	0.02%	1,690	0.01%	558	0..01%	1,409	0.01%
Rape[2]	215	0.01%	14,799	0.04%	6,583	0.03%	14,824	0.05%
Robbery	2,121	0.07%	52,301	0.13%	18,068	0.09%	28,988	1.00%
Aggravated assault	3,537	0.11%	105,541	0.27%	44,555	0.23%	76,253	0.26%
Property crime	22,441	0.70%	921,114	2.33%	267,155	1.37%	693,204	2.39%
Burglary	4,291	0.13%	152,555	0.39%	27,600	0.14%	113,902	0.39%
Larceny-theft	14,483	0.45%	626,802	1.59%	226,851	1.17%	501,813	1.73%
Motor vehicle theft	3,667	0.11%	141,757	0.36%	12,704	0.07%	77,489	0.27%

1 The violent crime figures include the offenses of murder, rape (revised definition), robbery, and aggravated assault.
2 The figures shown in this column for the offense of rape were estimated using the revised Uniform Crime Reporting (UCR) definition of rape. See data declaration for further explanation.

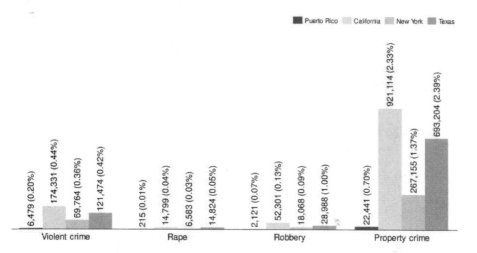

Things to Watch Out For

Petty theft can be a problem in Puerto Rico, so avoid drawing attention to yourself by wearing expensive clothing or accessories, and keep your belongings with you at all times. Try to blend in with the locals so you don't look like a tourist. If you can speak Spanish, now's the time to put your skills to use—English-speaking tourists are more likely to be targeted by pickpockets.

Puerto Rico has a fairly high homicide rate, but this shouldn't affect ordinary people, as it's almost entirely related to gang violence and drugs. As long as you stay out of gang areas, you should be fine. Public housing areas, called "caserios" by the locals, are also known for their high crime rates, particularly San Juan's Louis Lloren Torres. Other areas in San Juan to avoid at night include Piñones, Parque de las Palomas, La Perla, and Puerta de Tierra.

In contrast, Old San Juan, Isla Verde, Miramar, and Condado are considered some of the safest neighborhoods of San Juan at night and have regular police patrols. Bayamón and Dorado are also safe areas—our team lives in Condado, Bayamón, and Dorado. We have never experienced any problems here. If you have questions about these neighborhoods, don't hesitate to send us an email at info@relocatepuertorico.com.

We want to stress, though, that we are simply pointing out these problems so that you are aware of them. Puerto Rico is no more dangerous than any other U.S. city, and if you feel safe in the United States, you'll feel safe in Puerto Rico, too.

Hurricanes

An unfortunate reality of living in Puerto Rico is natural disasters, particularly hurricanes. The destruction the island sustained from Hurricanes Maria and Irma in 2017 is no secret. During hurricane season—June to November—keep an eye on the weather forecast, and take any warnings seriously. If a major hurricane strikes, you will probably lose power, so it's a good idea to buy a generator to power your fridge and other essential appliances.

You should always keep an emergency kit, too, just in case. Make sure to include a first-aid kit, any medications you might need to take, a device to communicate with your family, important documents (in a waterproof container), and a flashlight, among other things.

Earthquakes

Earthquakes are an additional threat to the otherwise peaceful life on this Caribbean island. All of Puerto Rico can experience strong earthquakes, although the island's west coast is most vulnerable. If you are from the West Coast of the United States, you're probably already familiar with how to deal with earthquakes, but if this isn't a hazard you have had to consider in the United States, here's an overview of measures you can take to protect yourself and your home.

To prepare your home for earthquakes, secure heavy appliances such as your fridge to the wall. Use wall studs to secure your water heater in place to avoid possible ruptures to gas and water connections. Secure expensive electronics and any valuable items to prevent falls or other damage. You can use anti-skid pads or Velcro to secure electronics like TVs and computers.

You should also set up your bedroom so you will be safe if an earthquake strikes in the middle of the night. Position your bed away from windows and chimneys, and keep the blinds or curtains shut at night to help prevent broken glass from falling on the bed. Avoid hanging pictures, light fixtures, or anything else that could fall above the bed.

During an earthquake, if you are inside, drop to the ground. Cover your head and take refuge under a table, desk, or other sturdy piece of furniture. Hold onto it so you aren't thrown around. If there is no suitable furniture to hide under, crouch against an interior wall. Do not attempt to leave the building—this is where many injuries occur. If you are outside during an earthquake, stay outside and distance yourself from any buildings. It's dangerous to be around exterior walls.

It's also important to avoid bookcases, tall furniture, and light fixtures during an earthquake, as they can fall on you. Avoid doors because they can slam shut suddenly, and avoid windows because they may break. Don't use the elevator during an earthquake, and if you are already in one when the earthquake strikes, get out as soon as possible. Avoid the coastline because dangerous tsunamis may occur.

Making Friends on the Island

Moving to an entirely new territory can be intimidating because it often means you're leaving behind your friends and family and going to a new place where you don't know anyone. Living in a new, unfamiliar location with no friends or acquaintances can quickly get lonely, and sometimes it's not easy to know how to make new friends. The good news is that there are hundreds of thousands of friendly local Puerto Ricans and fellow expatriates all across the island waiting to strike up a friendship with you. But how do you meet them?

Chat Groups

Whether it's WhatsApp or Discord, Internet users from around the world congregate in interest-based chat groups across different platforms. With most apps available on mobile and desktop, it's easy to connect with new people in Puerto Rico and start building your new circle of friends. Depending on the app, you may also be able to post pictures, videos, and Instagram- or Facebook-esque "stories." Most chat apps furthermore allow calls, often possible in groups.

In terms of chat group features, Discord generally reigns supreme, with its ability to partition discussions of particular topics to channels within the group. Whereas a WhatsApp chat group can be chaotic, a Discord chat group (termed "server") is usually far more organized, allowing users to easily ask specific questions or discuss certain topics.

Another advantage of Discord is that it has no limit on the number of users who can join a chat group. WhatsApp puts a cap on participant numbers, so many WhatsApp groups cannot accept new members until some existing ones leave.

Chat groups in Puerto Rico cover any number of topics and fields. Below are just a few examples—there's something for everyone.

Sports

There are sports groups for bowling, golf, soccer, basketball, volleyball, tennis, and even foosball—and those are in addition to the various fitness and wellness groups, including for acrobatics, yoga, dance, hiking, kickboxing, running, and rock climbing.

Hobbies

Are you a musician or a photographer? If so, there's a Puerto Rican chat group for you, too. There are also groups for bookworms, techno and EDM fans, tech geeks, crypto lovers, and board game aficionados.

Food

Whether you're a foodie looking for a dinner club or a vegan or vegetarian looking to meet like-minded Puerto Ricans, you can use chat applications to find new friends to eat with.

Lifestyle

There are groups for all different types of lifestyles, too, even relatively niche ones. There are groups for Christians, for biohackers, and for people in open or polyamorous relationships.

Work

If you're a female boss or entrepreneur and want to socialize with other businesswomen in Puerto Rico, the Ladies of Puerto Rico Discord group is for you. Having received overwhelmingly positive feedback, the group's carefully organized topic channels allow for streamlined communication with empowered Puerto Rican businesswomen. You can also find a group for coworking.

Puerto Rico–related

You can also find various groups related to facilitating your life in Puerto Rico. There's a group for housing and subletting, as well as one for practicing your Spanish language skills.

Get Links to Chat Groups in Puerto Rico

The important question you may be asking yourself now is how to join Puerto Rican chat groups. For both WhatsApp and Discord, you will need a link to the group, which, upon being clicked (or tapped, if you're on your phone), will lead you to a button to join the chat. For Discord, you can also navigate to the "+" icon at the bottom of the server list in the left-hand column. Hit "Add a Server," select "Join a server," paste the invite link, and hit "Join." If you would like the link to a particular group, please email gisela@relocatepuertorico.com and request it. Have fun with your new friends in Puerto Rico!

Frequently Asked Questions

Export Services Act Questions

What are eligible export services under Section 2031.01 of Act 60?

An Eligible Business shall be considered to qualify for the benefits of this Section, if the business has a bona fide office or establishment located in Puerto Rico that conducts the following service activities, within or outside of Puerto Rico, which, in turn, are considered Export Services or Promoter Services:

- Research and development
- Publicity and public relations
- Economic, environmental, technological, scientific, management, marketing, human resources, IT, and auditing consulting
- Advice on matters related to any industry or business
- Creative industries
- Production of construction plans, engineering and architecture services, and project management
- Professional services, such as legal, tax, and accounting services
- Centralized management services
- Electronic information processing center
- Development of computer programs
- The distribution of physical form, in the cyber network, by cloud computing, or as part of a blockchain network and the income from licensing, program subscriptions, or service charges
- Voice, video, audio, and data telecommunication to people located outside of Puerto Rico
- Call centers
- Shared services center
- Educational and training services
- Hospital and laboratory services, including medical tourism services and telemedicine facilities
- Investment banking and other financial services
- Marketing centers

What are the tax benefits of the Export Services tax incentive?

The primary benefits are as follows:
1. 4% corporate tax on income that is sourced from Puerto Rico by eligible businesses
2. 100% tax exemption on distributions to shareholders

When can I apply for the Export Services tax incentive?

You can apply for the Export Services Act at any time during the calendar year.

What is the process for applying for the Export Services tax incentive?

The individual needs to submit an application to the Office of Industrial Tax Exemption (OITE), which is a division of the Department of Economic Development and Commerce of Puerto Rico (DDEC).

How long does it take for an Export Services tax incentive application to be approved?

The amount of time varies based on the complexity of your business, the completeness of your application, and the staffing at the OITE. You should expect about six to eight months from application to confirmation.

How much does it cost to apply for the Export Services tax incentive?

- $1,000 application fee (does not include government fees related to business setup and compliance)

When is the start date for my Export Services decree?

The Export Services decree is retroactive to the date of filing, which happens just after your date of application.

Do I need to move to Puerto Rico for the Export Services Act?

No, the Export Services tax incentive is based on the business and not the individual. However, the Tax Cuts and Jobs Act of 2017 regarding retained earnings in controlled foreign corporations (CFCs) *may* disincentivize shareholders from living in the United States due to the mandatory repatriation of retained earnings, or a Global Intangible Low Tax Income (GILTI) tax. We recommend that any Export Services business shareholders relocate to Puerto Rico.

Who is eligible for the Export Services tax exemptions on distributions of dividends?

Shareholders, partners, and members of an eligible business who hold a decree shall not be subject to income tax on distributions of dividends.

What is a "reasonable salary" for the Export Services tax incentive?

Administrative Determination 15-22 requires you to pay yourself a reasonable salary based on the functions you perform for the company. Although there may be some rules of thumb, there is no precise formula. It is important to consider that AD 15-22 only requires a salary when you devote 80% or more of your time to working for the Export Services Act business.

When do I need a transfer pricing study to satisfy an "arm's length" transaction associated with my Export Services business?

You should consider a transfer pricing study a necessity if you will be doing business between your new Act 60 company and another entity with shared ownership. You should show intent by carrying out a transfer pricing analysis before starting a business with your new Export Services Act decree. Your intent could be an internal spreadsheet or a full $50,000+ study. If going at it alone, be sure to acknowledge accepted methodologies and risks to set yourself up for success.

Do I need to set up a bank account in Puerto Rico for the Export Services business?

No, but it is recommended for ease of doing business and residency purposes.

What are the annual filing requirements for the Export Services business?

1. All eligible businesses that hold a decree shall file an annual income tax return with the Secretary of the Treasury, regardless of their gross or net income and separate from any other return they are required to file.
2. Every shareholder or partner of an eligible business that holds a decree granted under this Act shall file an annual income tax return with the Department of the Treasury.
3. All eligible businesses that hold a decree shall annually file with the Exemption Office an authenticated report containing the signature of the Chair, managing partner, or authorized representative.

Can I transfer my Export Services Act decree?

Yes, but this requires the prior consent of the Secretary.

Do I need to start an LLC or business in Puerto Rico for the Export Services Act?

We recommend creating a new LLC for your application for ease of doing business and audit readiness.

Do I need the Investor Resident Individual tax decree in addition to an Export Services tax decree?

No, shareholders of an Export Services business will not be subject to income tax on distributions of dividends.

Investor Resident Individual Act Questions

When can I apply for the Investor Resident Individual tax incentive?

You can apply for the Investor Resident Individual tax incentive at any time during the calendar year, before or after you move to Puerto Rico. However, you must be a resident of Puerto Rico for your Investor Resident Individual decree to be effective.

How much does it cost to apply for the Investor Resident Individual tax incentive?[4]

- $750 application filing fee
- $50 acceptance filing fee
- ~$55 additional sworn statement filing fees
- $5,000 annual report filing fee
- $10,000 annual donation to nonprofit entities operating in Puerto Rico and are certified under Section 1101.01 of the Internal Revenue Code of Puerto Rico, which are not controlled by the same person who owns the Decree nor by their descendants or ascendants.

What is the process for applying for the Investor Resident Individual tax incentive?

The individual needs to submit an application to the Office of Industrial Tax Exemption (OITE), which is a division of the Department of Economic Development and Commerce of Puerto Rico (DDEC).

What are the tax benefits of the Investor Resident Individual tax incentive?

The benefits are as follows:

1. 100% exemption on capital gains tax for gains sourced (after you establish a tax home in Puerto Rico)
2. 100% exemption from interest and dividend income (for gains sourced from Puerto Rico-based payers)

What is Puerto Rico-sourced capital gains income?

Per the IRS, capital gains are sourced to the residence of the owner. Therefore, once an individual establishes their tax home in (relocates to) Puerto

---

[4] Fees may have increased as of the printing of this book so readers can email us for the current fee schedule.

Rico, any gains would be Puerto Rico-sourced and eligible for the Investor Resident Individual tax exemptions.

What is Puerto Rico-sourced interest and dividend income?

The source of income for dividends and interest is determined by the location of the payer. If the corporation is located in Delaware, it is U.S.-sourced income. If the corporation is located in Puerto Rico, it is Puerto Rico-sourced income. If you receive interest income from a U.S. payer, you may still owe the IRS taxes on that income, regardless of your place of residency.

How does being married impact the Investor Resident Individual requirements?

The bona fide residency rules pertaining to the Investor Resident Individual tax incentive are applied separately to each spouse. However, it is recommended that both spouses each obtain a separate Investor Resident Individual tax decree.

In the event that one spouse does not meet bona fide residency, only income attributable to the resident spouse will be entitled to the 933 Exclusion; other income will be subject to U.S. income taxes.

Can I apply the Investor Resident Individual tax exemptions to capital gains in my retirement accounts?

No, withdrawals from IRA, 401(k), and other U.S. tax-deferred retirement accounts are not covered by the Investor Resident Individual Act.

How long does it take for an Investor Resident Individual application to be approved?

The time for an Investor Resident Individual application takes about 60 days from application submission to acceptance.

How are capital gains on virtual currencies and stocks treated by the IRS?

In general, stocks and virtual currencies are treated as personal property for U.S. federal tax purposes. This means gains are allocated to the residence of the individual during which these gains were accrued.

Specifically, the sale or exchange of convertible virtual currency or the use of convertible virtual currency to pay for goods or services in a real-world economy transaction has tax consequences that may result in a tax liability.

When is my Investor Resident Individual decree active? How do my relocation date and my application date work together?

Key dates related to the Investor Resident Individual decree:

1. The date of establishing a tax home in Puerto Rico – this is critical for determining gains on popular types of capital gains, like stocks, as determined by the IRS.
2. Relocation date (same as #1)
3. Move date (same as #1)
4. Investor Resident Individual application date – the date you apply
5. Investor Resident Individual filing date – the date the OITE begins to formally review your application
6. Investor Resident Individual pre-acceptance date – the date you submit fees and notarized documents for an approved application
7. Investor Resident Individual acceptance date – the date you formally accept your decree

See our overview deck in the free downloads section, which includes an example of this topic.

How do I split a capital gain between appreciation before moving to Puerto Rico and after moving to Puerto Rico?

There are two types of investments:

1. Marketable investments (has a public market price) – note the investment price on the day you move to Puerto Rico. This is the date that bifurcates your gains.
2. Non-marketable investments (does not have a public market price) – using the "days of ownership" method, you would allocate your gains by dividing how many days in each jurisdiction you owned the asset.

What are the annual filings for the Investor Resident Individual decree?

There is an annual filing report that costs $5,000.

Does my spouse also need an Investor Resident Individual decree?

Yes, this is recommended.

Factors like community property and life events like divorce or death may complicate your scenario.

What is the difference between a marketable and non-marketable security?

Marketable security

- Marketable securities are financial instruments and foreign currencies that are actively traded and liquid. An example would be a public stock.

Non-marketable security

- Non-marketable securities are usually U.S. Savings Bonds and private shares. Individuals cannot sell these types of securities to another investor. An example here would be a business interest in a private company, which may or may not have a fair market value (FMV) established.

If I'm expecting a future company liquidity event, can I benefit from the Investor Resident Individual tax incentive?

Yes. In general, you want to move to Puerto Rico, apply for the Investor Resident Individual tax incentive, and exercise your shares as soon as possible. If you own substantial restricted stock units (RSUs), your upside may be limited.

If you've already exercised shares, moving to Puerto Rico quickly is important because non-marketable share taxes are determined based on the amount of days you've lived in different jurisdictions.

Residency Questions

What is the "Year of the Move" rule?

You will satisfy the tax home and closer connection tests in the tax year of changing your residence to Puerto Rico if you meet all of the following:

- You have not been a bona fide resident of Puerto Rico in any of the three tax years immediately preceding your move.
- In the year of the move, you do not have a tax home outside Puerto Rico or a closer connection to the United States or a foreign country than to Puerto Rico during any of the last 183 days of the tax year.
- You are a bona fide resident of Puerto Rico for each of the three tax years immediately following your move.

What is the presence test?

If you are a U.S. citizen or resident alien, you will satisfy the presence test for the entire tax year if you meet one of the following conditions:

1. You were present in Puerto Rico for at least 183 days during the tax year.
2. You were present in Puerto Rico for at least 549 days during the three-year period that includes the current tax year and the two immediately preceding tax years. During each year of the three-year period, you must be present in Puerto Rico for at least 60 days.
3. You were present in the United States for no more than 90 days during the tax year.
4. You earned income in the United States of no more than a total of $3,000 and were present for more days in Puerto Rico than in the United States during the tax year. Earned income is pay for personal services performed, such as wages, salaries, or professional fees.
5. You had no significant connection to the United States during the tax year.

What is a tax home?

You will have met the tax home test if you did not have a tax home outside Puerto Rico during any part of the tax year.

Your tax home is your regular or main place of business, employment, or post of duty regardless of where you maintain your family home. If you do not have a regular or main place of business because of the nature of your work, then your tax home is the place where you regularly live. If you do not fit either of these categories, you are considered an itinerant, and your tax home is wherever you work.

What is a closer connection?

You will have met the closer connection test if, during any part of the tax year, you do not have a closer connection to the United States or a foreign country than to Puerto Rico.

You will be considered to have a closer connection to Puerto Rico than to the United States or to a foreign country if you have maintained more significant connections with Puerto Rico than with the United States or foreign country. In determining if you have maintained more significant connections with Puerto Rico, the facts and circumstances to be considered include but are not limited to the following:

- The location of your permanent home
- The location of your family
- The location of personal belongings, such as automobiles, furniture, clothing, and jewelry owned by you and your family
- The location of social, political, cultural, professional, or religious organizations with which you have a current relationship
- The location where you conduct your routine personal banking activities
- The location where you conduct business activities (other than those that go into determining your tax home)
- The location of the jurisdiction in which you hold a driver's license
- The location of the jurisdiction in which you vote
- The location of charitable organizations to which you contribute
- The country of residence you designate on forms and documents
- The types of official forms and documents you file, such as Form W-8BEN or Form W-9

Do I need to sell my home in the United States?

While this is recommended, it is not required. This is only one component of the closer connection test.

As a rule of thumb, ensure the location of your permanent home is in Puerto Rico. You could also rent your U.S. home.

What is Form 8898?

Use Form 8898 to notify the IRS that you have become or ceased to be a bona fide resident of a U.S. possession. The information you provide on this form is specific and important to executing a relocation to Puerto Rico.

What if I am a green card holder?

A holder of a green card is treated as a U.S. resident and is subject to the same taxes as any other U.S. citizen.

Puerto Rico Questions

What is a U.S. possession or territory?

U.S. territories are islands under the jurisdiction of the United States. U.S. possessions can be divided into two groups:

1. Those that have their own governments and their own tax systems (Puerto Rico, U.S. Virgin Islands, Guam, American Samoa, and The Commonwealth of the Northern Mariana Islands).
2. Those that do not have their own governments or their own tax systems (Midway Island, Wake Island, Palmyra Island, Howland Island, Johnston Island, Baker Island, Kingman Reef, Jarvis Island, and other U.S. islands, cays, and reefs that are not part of any of the 50 states).

Are Puerto Rican residents U.S. citizens?

Yes, in 1917, the U.S. Congress passed the Jones-Shafroth Act, which grants U.S. citizenship to anyone born on the island.

Is a passport needed to travel to Puerto Rico?

No, you can expect the same travel requirements and TSA restrictions as when traveling within the mainland.

How much does it cost to ship my vehicle to Puerto Rico?

There are multiple factors involved that will determine your exact cost. You can get an online quote from a vehicle shipping service such as Puerto Rico Car Transport.

The Puerto Rican government also charges a tax based on the value of the vehicle.

Does Puerto Rico pay U.S. taxes?

Because Puerto Rico is a U.S. territory, only government employees pay federal income tax. All other employers and employees pay no federal income taxes. Residents of Puerto Rico do pay federal payroll taxes, such as Social Security and Medicare taxes.

Employers in Puerto Rico are subject to both Federal Insurance Contributions Act (FICA) tax and the Federal Unemployment Tax Act (FUTA).

Puerto Rico imposes a separate income tax in lieu of federal income tax.

Are banks in Puerto Rico FDIC insured?

Yes, FDIC deposit insurance covers the depositors of a failed FDIC-insured bank for up to at least $250,000.

What is the expatriation/repatriation tax when moving to/from Puerto Rico?

There is no expatriation, or exit tax, when moving to Puerto Rico. This can be as high as 23.8% on all assets for other jurisdictions.

For repatriation, as long as you earn this income as a Puerto Rico resident, there are no taxes. This money can be transferred freely. If you are not a resident, this would be tax deferral, and there would be a tax when/if you bring it back to the mainland. One option to avoid this tax would be to invest it offshore or to become a Puerto Rico resident and claim it tax-free.

Is Puerto Rico safe?

Puerto Rico, as of 2019, was generally safer than other U.S. states. Our take is that if you exercise caution, as you would in any major U.S. city, you will minimize your chances of being targeted by mostly opportunistic crime. The area where you live will determine the crime rates.

How much does it cost to move to Puerto Rico?

You can expect normal relocation costs, like license and vehicle registration, as you would for an interstate move. If you plan on transporting items like a car and personal belongings, shipping and possible excise costs will significantly increase the amount you spend. Fortunately, air travel and flight prices are comparable to U.S. transcontinental routes.

Which key documents do I need to bring with me to Puerto Rico?

You should bring all key identification and tax documents to Puerto Rico. This will ensure you are prepared in the event of an audit.

At a minimum, you should bring the following for the purposes of tax applications and registrations:

1. Passport
2. Original social security card
3. Current driver's license

Note: A birth certificate is not required.

Where are popular places to live in Puerto Rico?

Here are a few of the most popular places to live for relocating individuals:

- Old San Juan (OSJ) – old-city living in San Juan
- Condado / Miramar – high-rise living in San Juan
- Ocean Park – residential living in San Juan
- Bayamon / Guaynabo – suburban living 10 minutes south of San Juan
- Dorado – gated golfing community 30 minutes west of San Juan
- Palmas del Mar – boating suburb 60 minutes southeast of San Juan

Can a U.S. citizen buy property in Puerto Rico?

Yes, although you can expect a slightly more complicated process and a longer timeline. Real property in Puerto Rico is governed by property laws of Puerto Rico.

How much does a house cost in Puerto Rico?

Check Zillow or another online platform for current home prices. We can help in recommending a realtor since properties are not always listed online or in a centralized MLS system.

Do homeowners in Puerto Rico pay property taxes?

Yes, property taxes are based on the last national appraisal in 1958 and are usually lower than most U.S. states (about 0.5% annually of property value).

Do residents of Puerto Rico file federal tax returns?

If you're a bona fide resident of Puerto Rico during the entire tax year, you generally aren't required to file a U.S. federal income tax return if your only income is from sources within Puerto Rico. If you're a bona fide resident of Puerto Rico and a U.S. government employee, you must file a U.S. income tax return. Residents of Puerto Rico pay federal payroll taxes, including Social Security and Medicare taxes, just as residents of the States do.

How much are personal and corporate income tax rates in Puerto Rico?

Personal

The island imposes a separate local Puerto Rico income tax in place of typical U.S. federal income tax. The personal income tax rate in Puerto Rico is

33% for net taxable income over $61,500. This is applicable to wages regardless of whether one has an Export Services decree or Investor Resident Individual decree.

Corporate

The corporate income tax rate is 39% (without tax incentives).

Will I owe self-employment tax if I live in Puerto Rico?

Yes, bona fide residents of a U.S. territory who have self-employment income must generally pay self-employment tax to the United States. Self-employment tax includes both Social Security and Medicare.

Self-employment tax is money that a small business owner must pay to the federal government to fund Medicare and Social Security. Self-employment tax is due when an individual has net earnings of $400 or more in self-employment income over the course of the tax year. In any business, both the company and the employee are taxed to pay for these two major social welfare programs. When an individual is self-employed, he or she is both the company and the employee, so he or she pays both shares of this tax.

What are the current Puerto Rico income tax brackets?

Net taxable income (USD)	Tax
Not over 9,000	0%
Over 9,000, but not over 25,000	7% of the excess over USD 9,000
Over 25,000, but not over 41,500	USD 1,120 plus 14% of the excess over USD 25,000
Over 41,500, but not over 61,500	USD 3,430 plus 25% of the excess over USD 41,500
Over 61,500	USD 8,430 plus 33% of the excess over USD 61,500

Other Questions

What is a controlled foreign corporation (CFC)?

A controlled foreign corporation (CFC) is any corporation organized outside the United States (a foreign corporation) that is more than 50% owned by U.S. shareholders.

CFC rules are designed to limit tax deferral by using offshore low-taxed entities. These rules concern the income of an entity that is not currently taxed to the owner of the entity.

What is the global intangible low-taxed income tax (GILTI)?

The Tax Cuts and Jobs Act of 2017 (TCJA) imposes a special tax on global intangible low-taxed income (GILTI). Generally, this tax is at a 10.5% rate on a U.S. shareholder's share of a CFC's GILTI.

The GILTI tax became effective for taxable years beginning January 1, 2018.

How is divorce treated for decree holders?

You must have been a resident of Puerto Rico for one year to file for divorce in Puerto Rico. In general, Puerto Rico courts split assets 50/50; therefore, you must consider what leaving Puerto Rico will do to your residency status.

What is the Foreign Earned Income Exclusion (FEIE)?

If you work and reside outside the United States and meet either the Bona Fide Resident or Physical Presence test (these tests are defined differently from those for Puerto Rico), you're eligible to exclude up to $108,700 in foreign earned income as of the 2021 tax year.

This strategy would be an alternative to Puerto Rico-based tax incentives. When pursued in a country with a low or non-existent tax rate, an individual could see a large tax advantage on the FEIE amount.

Which annual tax filings are required for individuals living in Puerto Rico?

Annual income tax

- U.S. residents need to file a 1040 U.S. Individual Income Tax Return
- Bona fide Puerto Rico residents need to file a 482 Puerto Rico Income Tax Return

Annual self-employment tax

- Both U.S. and Puerto Rico residents need to file a self-employment tax return (Form 1040)

What is the municipal license tax rate in Puerto Rico?

The volume of business tax is between 0.2% and 0.5% of sales volume. Some municipalities give additional discounts.

What is the sales tax rate, or IVU, in Puerto Rico?

The Sales and Use Tax (SUT) is 11.5%; 10.5% is imposed by Puerto Rico's Department of Treasury, while the additional percent goes to municipalities.

What is a registered agent?

A registered agent is a responsible third party who is registered in the same state in which a business entity was established and who is designated to receive service of process notices, correspondence from the Secretary of State, and other official government notifications, usually tax forms and notice of lawsuits, on behalf of the corporation or LLC.

If you do not have a physical location in the state in which your business is registered, you must select a registered agent to accept documents on your behalf. Puerto Rico needs to know it has a contact person for your business within the state at all times. P.O. boxes are not acceptable addresses for registered agents.

What is a Merchant's Number Certification?

This number is the official registry in the Department of the Treasury for all natural or juridical persons who do or wish to do business in Puerto Rico. The fines for not registering in the Department of Treasury can be up to $10,000.

What is a Use Permit, or "Carta de Consulta"?

Prior to applying for the municipal license, you need to apply for the Use Permit from the Municipality of San Juan, which is approved by the Permits Office of San Juan.

What is a municipal license, or "Patente Municipal"?

This license is required in order to start a business in a municipality. A corporation engaged in trade or business in Puerto Rico is normally subject to the payment of municipal license taxes. The tax rate varies depending on the gross income but ranges from 0.2% to 0.5% of revenue.

Am I still eligible for Act 60 if I was previously arrested or if my background check shows criminal activity?

As of November 2021, PRelocate has not had any clients rejected for Act 60 for a background check issue. Several PRelocate clients who have had DUIs, restraining orders, or drug charges have been approved. However, while there is no specific published list of crimes or issues that would render an applicant ineligible for Act 60, Act 60 decrees are given at the discretion of the Head of the Department of Economic Development and Commerce (DDEC) who oversees the Puerto Rico Act 60 program.